Edward Clark Lunt

The present condition of economic science and the demand
for a radical change in its methods and aims

Edward Clark Lunt

The present condition of economic science and the demand for a radical change in its methods and aims

ISBN/EAN: 9783337118181

Printed in Europe, USA, Canada, Australia, Japan

Cover: Foto ©Suzi / pixelio.de

More available books at **www.hansebooks.com**

THE PRESENT CONDITION

OF

ECONOMIC SCIENCE

AND THE

DEMAND FOR A RADICAL CHANGE

IN ITS

METHODS AND AIMS

BY

EDWARD CLARK LUNT, A.M.

"Hold fast that which is good."—*1 Thessalonians, v., 21*
"Striving to better, oft we mar what's well."—*King Lear*

NEW YORK AND LONDON
G. P. PUTNAM'S SONS
The Knickerbocker Press
1888

ANALYTICAL TABLE OF CONTENTS.

I.

GENERAL BILL OF ATTAINDER AGAINST ECONOMICS. 1–6

Political economy ever distrusted, and economic writers always at variance, 1—Signs of revolt in recent years more rife than ever, 2–3—Daniel Webster "gives up" political economy; so do Carlyle, Laveleye, Jevons, and others, 4—Logic under the same cloud of popular disfavor, but the case of economics peculiarly unpromising, 5–6.

II.

PRESENT CONDITION OF ECONOMICS LUDICROUSLY INHARMONIOUS . . . 7–12

Economic controversies, from one point of view, highly entertaining, 7–8—The average economist the prince of polemics, 9–10—Economic disputants more remarkable for their *fortiter in re* than for their *suaviter in modo*, 11—Notwithstanding this formidable introduction, the author espouses the cause of the current economics, 12—And, as a necessary part of his defence, ventures an

III.

EXPLANATION OF THE PRESENT ILL-REPUTE
OF ECONOMICS 13-42

General misunderstanding of the aims and the province of political economy, 13-22—Economics as a science—a systematized body of knowledge: not an assemblage of rules aiming at practical ends, 13-14 [Note: Harvard College and free-trade, 14-15.]—Nevertheless, all economists concern themselves with practical questions, 16—And may properly do so in view of the distinction between pure and applied science, 17—Failure to make this distinction injures economics in two ways: (*a*) by requiring too much of the science, 18; (*b*) by estranging the working classes, 19-20—The foregoing view of economics not over-ambitious, but the only view consistent with the scientific character of the study, 21—A second reason for the disrepute of political economy found in the anarchical condition of the economic world, 22-29—Diverting psychological study presented by the wages-fund controversy, 23-24—Still, the condition of economics is less chaotic than would appear at the first blush: a large part of the controversies are either insignificant or connected with the applications of economics, 25-26 —Certain controversies, however, are more formidable, since they concern fundamental questions in the science, 27—But even these graver differences may be adjusted: *cf.*, for example, a possible solution of the wages-fund controversy, 28-29—Another thing to be noted in connection with the reputation of economics—the astonishing incompetence of critics, 30—Why political economy, more than other subjects, suffers from this cause, 31—The supposed pessimistic tone of economic doctrines an-

Analytical Table of Contents. v

other reason for the ill-favor of economics, 32–37—How far can apparent resulting harmonies be taken as attesting the truth of economic doctrines? 33—The example of Carey and Bastiat in this respect, 34—Some foundation for the common reproach in the heavy-hearted views of early economists: *cf.* Malthus and Sismondi, 35—But the absurdity of this reproach follows from the fact that political economy is a *science:* if economics is the "dismal," where is the "blithesome" science? 36–37—Still another cause of the unpopularity of economics is found in the fact that men's personal interests are directly touched by the science, 38—A final cause more reasonable than some of the preceding—the mistakes of economists, 39—Grotesquely erroneous doctrines once taught by political economy, 41 [Note: Sismondi and general over-production. Sismondi's error, under the circumstances, a very natural one, 40]—The ground now cleared for the second part of our subject—the "demand for a radical change," 42—Various names by which this demand is known: "German," "Realistic," "Inductive," and "Historical," 42—Persistent misrepresentation making necessary a

IV.

GENERAL STATEMENT OF THE ENGLISH METHOD 43–51

Axiomatic mental principles and undeniable physical conditions made the basis of deductive reasoning, 44—This reasoning corrected and supplemented by the inductive tests of economic history, 45—The inductive element, though frequently overlooked by critics, an essential part of the English method, 46—Singular misconceptions of English doctrines vi *Analytical Table of Contents.*

PAGE

in current criticisms, 46-48—Mr. J. R. Ingram affords a notable example, 49-50—The new economics more disposed to pull down than to build up, 51—So that we may conveniently begin our exposition of Historical doctrines by examining

V.

THE NEGATIVE SIDE OF THE NEW SCHOOL, 52-73

The first criticism—that the English method is exclusively deductive—based on a mistaken idea of that method, 52-57—German economists not agreed as to the place of deduction in economic research: *cf.* Schmoller and Wagner, 52—Disagreement, too, on this point among the English adherents of the new school: *cf.* Leslie and Ingram, 54-55—The theory of the English method calls for the constant use of induction, 56—And practice has conformed to the theory, 57 [Note: Ricardo largely responsible for this criticism, 56.]—A second criticism based on the alleged absolute character of the English doctrines, 57-63—In point of fact, economic principles are closely related to circumstances of time and place, 58—A truth that the new economists proclaim with a great flourish of trumpets, 59 —But the old economists never supposed any thing else the case, 60—As the words of Mill, Bagehot, and others evince, 61—In fact, this truth is implied in the logical method of the English school, 62—The whole thing of theoretical, rather than of practical, importance: economics virtually the same the world over, 63 — Another criticism alleges that the English political economy places too much dependence upon competition, 63-68—Combination, no doubt, an increasingly important factor in the solution of industrial problems, 64-65—This

Analytical Table of Contents. vii

possibility provided for in the theory of the English economics, 66—And the fact fully recognized in the practice of English economists, 67—Still another criticism arraigns the English school for its attitude toward the doctrine of *laissez-faire*, 68–72 —Thereby exemplifying the logical fallacy of *ignoratio elenchi*, 68—The economic world vastly changed since Adam Smith so strongly recommended this doctrine, 69—And perhaps a corresponding change should be made in applied economics, 70— But the whole thing is irrelevant to our present inquiry, since the doctrine of *laissez-faire* forms no essential part of English economics, 71—The foregoing are the leading features in the critical aspect of the new economists. Unnumbered minor criticisms need not check our progress toward (72–73)

VI.

THE POSITIVE SIDE OF THE NEW SCHOOL, 74-101

Insistence upon the use of history the leading feature of the new method, 74—One way of using history—Schmoller's way—already discredited in these pages, and, indeed, repudiated by most Historical economists, 75—Another and more temperate use of history made by Wagner, 76—His "Historical" method hardly distinguishable from the "Orthodox" method, 77—In fact, the English method itself is historical, 78—As the practice of Smith, Malthus, Mill, and others shows, 79 —And is not called "Historical" only because of the greater importance of the deductive element, 80—Examination of Professor Smith's contention that history can supply economics with general principles, 81 [Note: The folly of ascribing general business conditions to one or another kind of tariff policy, 82.] — Historical economists, however, invariably take their general principles from the " Orthodox " collection, 83—Thus, so far as its leading feature is concerned, the new method is not new, 84—But the Historical school has a good title to novelty in merging economics in the general science of sociology, 85-91—The English conception of the relation between economics and associated subjects, 86 — Historical statements of the new doctrine full of " glittering generalities," and greatly in need of specific examples, 87-88—A simple illustration shows the value of the English method in this respect, 89-90—Practice, reason, and analogy all against the new view, 91—A third positive characteristic of the new school found in the attempted " reunion of ethics with political economy," 92-96—Ethical interests not neglected in the English method, 93 — Impracticability of including in one science moral and economic considerations, 94 — Examples illustrative of this, 95 — A final positive feature of the new school found in its advocacy of paternal government, 96-101—Little here to detain us, since economics is not concerned with political theories, 97—The tendency toward government tutelage much aggravated in this country by the civil war, 98—Warning notes from authoritative voices, 99-100.

VII.

THE RESULTS OF OUR STUDY . . . 102–114

The chief result seems to be the demonstration of the fact that the new school lacks one great essential — a *raison d'être*, 102 — This conclusion suggested by the theory of the new school, and confirmed by the works of that school, 103—Great achievements of the English economics, 104 [Note: Adam Smith more fortunate than most social reformers in securing a speedy recognition of his doctrines, 104.]—The issue of this struggle between the schools easy to foresee, 106-107—No good reasons why economists should not join their forces, and thus more effectively undertake the work before them, 108—Extent and importance of this work; unnumbered economic problems clamoring for attention, 109 — These questions especially grave in this country, 110—Our singular indifference in the past to economic science, 111-112—And consequent advisability now of wasting no time over theoretical questions of method, 113-114.

BIRD'S-EYE VIEW OF THIS ESSAY.

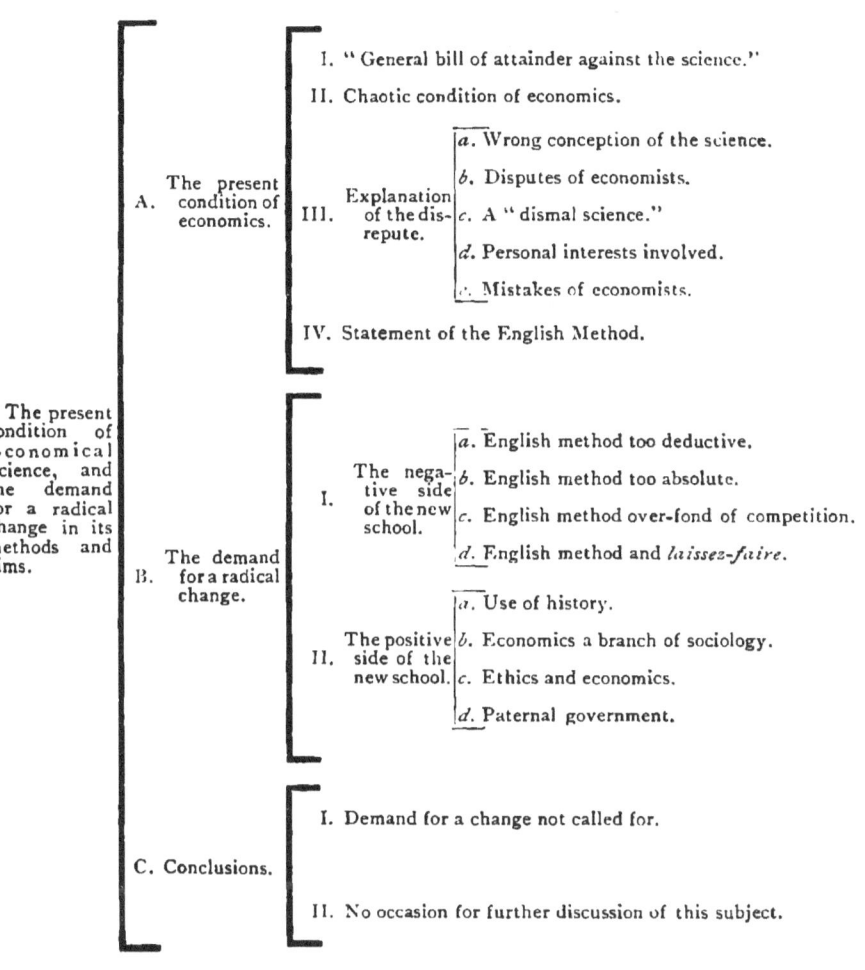

THE PRESENT CONDITION OF ECONOMICAL SCIENCE, AND THE DEMAND FOR A RADICAL CHANGE IN ITS METHODS AND AIMS.

I.

"GENERAL BILL OF ATTAINDER THAT HAS BEEN BROUGHT AGAINST THE SCIENCE AT LARGE."

The present condition of economic science is a thing to be spoken of with bated breath. At no period have the doctrines of political economy shared largely in the public confidence; and in recent years this disrepute has become increasingly prevalent. In 1821, as Professor Cairnes has pointed out, Colonel Torrens prophesied a speedy end to economic controversies: "In the progress of the human mind, a period of controversy amongst the cultivators of any branch of science must necessarily precede the period of unanimity. With respect to Political Economy, the period of controversy is passing away, and that of unanimity rapidly approaching. Twenty years hence there will scarcely exist a doubt respecting any of its fundamental principles."[1] Alas for human foresight! Thrice twenty years have passed since this unhappy prophecy was made, and yet to-day the "period of unanimity" seems more remote than ever, and the fundamental principles are hedged about with the gravest kind of doubt. The law of production from the soil, the theory of population, the effects of foreign trade, the law of rent, the theory of wages —these and other vital questions in economic science must even now be regarded as moot-points.

The effect of this uncertainty as to fundamental matters, is clearly seen in the wide-spread distrust of political economy. Everywhere the doctrines of the science are received with the utmost scepticism. A few years ago the proposition was made to remove economics from its place in the

[1] "Essay on the Production of Wealth," p. xiii. [1821].

course of the British Association for the Advancement of Science, on the ground that economic science had never shown itself worthy of the name. According to Macleod, "The political economy of Adam Smith, Ricardo, and Mill is now exhausted—it is a *caput mortuum* from which no further good can be extracted: it is wholy incapable of grasping the great economic problems of the day."[1] In 1876, when the Political Economy Club of England gave a centenary dinner commemorating the birth of economics with the publication of the "Wealth of Nations," the newspapers hinted that the economists might more properly solemnize the obsequies of their science. A recent writer in the *North American Review* declares that "the works of Malthus, Ricardo, and Mill are read, not so much because they teach us truth, as because they stand as mile-posts which serve to measure the distance by which thought has passed them." Forty years ago Carlyle was moved to admonish professors of econom-

[1] "Elements of Economics," p. v.

ics in this way : " Soft you a little . . . I preceive that the length of your tether is pretty well run, and that I must request you to talk a little lower in the future."[1] Some time after this, M. Laveleye apparently preceived that the "length of their tether" was completely run, and declared that "political economy, the old orthodox political economy of the Smiths, the Says, and the Bastiats, is dead, has closed its life, and the sentence of death appears perfectly legitimate." According to Ruskin, the acceptance of the current doctrines of political economy is a standing disgrace to the human intellect. Mr. Stanley Jevons despairs of progress under existing methods, affirming that "the only hope of attaining a true system of economics is to fling aside, once and forever, the mazy and preposterous assumptions of the Ricardian school." Daniel Webster has recourse to arithmetic, and finds that, if we take from political economy first all the truisms and then all the doubtful points, our remainder will be a quantity closely

[1] "Latter-Day Pamphlets," pp. 38, 39.

approximating zero; and he echoes the general opinion in these words: "I give up what is called the science of political economy. There is no such science. There are no rules on these subjects so fixed and invariable that their aggregate constitutes a science."

The only study at all comparable in this respect with political economy is logic. Logic shares with economics the contempt of the vulgar, and the hesitating, half-hearted support of the learned. "Did God make man two-legged and leave it to Aristotle to make him rational?"[1] triumphantly queries the logical scoffer; and in the same breath the "professorial dicta of so-called economists" are held up to scorn. But logic has this advantage over political economy: the students of logic believe in the science, however much heretics may deride the snaring subtleties of the syllogism. Yet, even those most devoted to economic research are distrustful of their science. Mr. Bagehot admits[2] that polit-

[1] *Cf.* Locke: "Of Human Understanding," Book iv., chap. 17, sec. 4.
[2] "Economic Studies," p. 3.

ical economy "lies rather dead in the public mind. Not only does it not excite the same interest as formerly, but there is not exactly the same confidence in it." Professor Dunbar complains[1] that his countrymen, after a century of remarkable intellectual activity in other departments of science, have added nothing to political economy. Bonamy Price calls his chosen field of work "the mysterious region of political economy." Professor Cairnes in various places adds to the gospel of economic discontent, affirming that political economy has "no small proportion of faulty material," lamenting "the confusion and contradictions in which the science is involved," and acknowledging that the study of his life is everywhere regarded with "profound distrust."

[1] *North American Review*, Jan., 1876.

II.

THE PRESENT CONDITION OF ECONOMICS LUDICROUSLY INHARMONIOUS.

In every science some doctors disagree; but in political economy few doctors agree, and the phrase "jargon of the schools" has especial significance. " Nothing can be more astonishing or lamentable," says Macleod,[1] "than the difference of doctrines, and the antagonism of economists on almost every point in the science." This statement is grievously near the truth; but we have a crumb of comfort in the fact that, besides being astonishing and lamentable, this "antagonism of economists" is at times infinitely diverting. What student of political economy has not shuddered at the sanguinary battles of the economic books? Indeed, the economist going forth to battle with his peers is a

[1] "Elements of Economics," p. vi.

truly formidable creature. In his right hand he carries the lance of excoriating satire, in his left the shield of unmeasured invective. Below are the greaves of vituperative epithet, and above the helmet of stinging sarcasm. His steed sniffs contention from afar, and leaps at the prospect of a scurrilous engagement.

It should be said, however, that for the most part our economic warriors are content to use the lighter weapons,—to shoot the arrows of insinuation rather than hurl the battle-axe of textual expression. The economic disputant commonly begins by "venturing to dissent" from his distinguished opponents; a little further on, he makes bold to hazard the conjecture that possibly his opponents are without some of the qualifications essential to success in economic research ; and, finally, he shows beyond a shadow of doubt that the position taken by his opponents is utterly repugnant to common sense and reason, and could be defended only by those from whose cerebral furniture nature had withheld some essential appointment. Usually, to be sure, the way in which our economist hints at the incompleteness of his opponent's mental outfit is the perfection of controversial manner; but, after all, Ophelia's words stand out unmistakably between the lines :

> " Now see that noble and most sovereign reason,
> Like sweet bells jangled out of tune, and harsh."

Indeed, what masterly polemics the least of economists are ! They have the richest vocabulary of qualifying words ; and skilfully attaching these to propositions as " broad and general as the casing air," they commit themselves to no more than they cannot help. How artfully they hedge their statements ; and what a wealth of saving clauses they have formed—" in the absence of disturbing causes," " generally and somewhat elliptically speaking," " modified by a rough, conjectural allowance," " the average results of the general actions of great bodies of men." They are always calling our attention to suppositional cases, fearing, as Bagehot says,[1]

[1] "Economic Studies," p. 18.

to cite instances near at hand, lest those same instances should be turned against them. They have the most lynx-eyed vision for incongruities and the most scathingly satirical way of holding them up to view. They delight to "cavil on the ninth part of a hair," and would delight still more, if the division were finer. They are constitutionally opposed to assenting in any form, even "with civil leer"; but whoever would acquire the utmost facility in "damning with faint praise" should give his days and nights to the volumes of economic writers. Pick up the economic treatise that lies nearest at hand, and you will find it full of passages like these: "Such a tissue of contradictions and inconsistencies"; "If I may venture to conjecture the meaning of this remarkable passage (which has a curiously Hibernian ring about it), possibly what Mr. —— *meant* to say was," etc.; "His ignorance [an obscure Englishman, John Ruskin by name, is the person referred to] of the doctrines and works which he undertakes to refute is not only extensive and profound, but curiously exact and minute."

Sometimes our economists are even less mindful of the *suaviter in modo ;* and when they do open the flood-gates of their invective, it is time for fastidious people to move on. These are some of the honey-mouthed phrases that they offer to ears polite : " The most ludicrous misconception," "pestilent heresy," "bestial idiotism." Horace Greeley, with characteristic fervor of language, used to call his economic adversaries "blear-eyed pedants." He whom some are pleased to denominate " the leading American economist" was noted for his warmth of feeling : Mr. Carey, we are told, "sometimes clinched his deliverances with expletives and epithets somewhat out of fashion in society "; and another observer declares that Carey swore like a bargeman whenever Mill's name was mentioned.

So much for one view of the present condition of economic science. The picture of that condition as here presented is by no means a flattering one. In all these quoted opinions there has been no lack of accentuation ; and nothing would be easier than the multiplication of such quotations. Still, there is something to be said on the other side of the question ; and in the rest of this essay the attempt will be made to present that other side, and to show that the present condition of the science, bad as that condition undoubtedly is in some respects, is yet not altogether hopeless, and, at all events, is not likely to be improved by the methods commonly recommended for that purpose. It is not, perhaps, the part of a good advocate to present the worst side of his case at the start ; but a just cause can afford to neglect the arts of the court-room, and will deem judicial impartiality of the first importance. Since, however, we have called attention so pointedly to this wide-spread distrust of economics, it behooves us, if we are to justify the pretensions of existing methods, to account satisfactorily for this notable disrepute ; and it is to that task, accordingly, that we will now address ourselves.

III.

EXPLANATION OF THE PRESENT ILL-REPUTE OF ECONOMICS.

A fundamental cause of the dark clouds of distrust with which the economic sky is now overcast may be found in the widely current misconception of the aims and the province of political economy. What the function of the science is becomes clear when we remember that political economy *is* a science ; for science is defined as " knowledge that is its own end," that is to say, knowledge that does not aim at a practical end. The object of a science is to get knowledge, to discover laws, to ascertain the causal connection between phenomena ; and the object of economic science is to discover the laws underlying the production and the distribution of wealth—to ascertain what economic effects follow what economic causes.

So much and so much only does political economy, as a science, set before itself. Accordingly, economics, conceived in this way, does not say that free trade is a better commercial policy than protection ; but the science does declare that international exchanges of commodities take place only when economy of production would be thereby promoted ; and a legislator might, under conceivable circumstances, deduce from this scientific fact some such practical conclusion as the foregoing.[1] In like manner political economy

[1] Some people seem to think that there are two sciences of political economy, one teaching free trade and the other protection. This is the view, apparently, of a certain Boston editor, a believer in protection, who advised a friend of the writer's not to study political economy at Harvard College, because "they do not teach it properly there." Of course, there can be no question as to the impropriety of using the prestige of a professorial chair for the purpose either of aiding or of opposing a political movement. What the editor had in mind when he gave the foregoing advice was the attitude of the economic department at Harvard on the question of free trade ; but, if I may judge from a somewhat intimate acquaintance with that department, his strictures were utterly unfounded. Having sat for four years under one of the leading professors of economics at Harvard College, I think I do not exaggerate in saying that never in all this time has he delivered a sentence from the lecturer's platform that would positively identify him with any particular commercial

is absolutely dumb when asked whether communism or private property is the better institution; though here again the science will at once respond when questioned about the ascertained laws underlying these different systems of distribution. "The economist's conclusions," says Senior, "do not authorize him in adding a syllable of advice"; a proceeding that would be a simple impertinence in view of the fact that the scientist's business is, not to give advice, but to seek and to ascertain truth. In fine, political economy is not moral nor social philosophy, nor legislation, nor yet the science of government.

Political economy is none of these; and insistence upon this fact is, as we shall try to show in a moment, not wholly uncalled for. But it will not do to leave the matter here; for the question at once arises, How is it, then, that so large a part of the books on economics is taken up with discussions of these practical matters? All

policy. Of course, there have not been wanting inferential evidences of his views; but it has always been the economist, and never the politician—always the judge, and never the advocate,—that has occupied the academic chair.

economists, from Adam Smith, who made his book a mighty engine for the overthrow of the mercantile system, to the present American economists, who are battling for a liberalized tariff, have aimed at practical ends; that is, have concerned themselves with questions not strictly within the domain of political economy.

There are two ways in which to defend this conduct. Cicero, in a familiar passage, declares that all studies pertaining to liberal knowledge are united by a certain tie of kinship; and in the case of the social sciences this "*quoddam commune vinculum*" is especially binding. This mutuality and close interrelation of social studies seems to some economists a sufficient justification for the introduction of practical questions into their books; but a more secure warrant for such a proceeding is indicated by Mill, when he calls his book: "The Principles of Political Economy: *with Some of Their Applications to Social Philosophy*." The clause of this title that I have italicized shows the ground upon which an economist has a right to deal with practical questions—a right based on the distinction between the pure or applied science and applied arts. Just as the science of astronomy furnishes material for the art of navigation; just as the science of geometry is the basis for the applied arts of surveying and engineering : so the abstract science of political economy furnishes data to be utilized in the arts of taxation, banking, and so on.

"All this is true enough," says some demurring reader, "but what is the use of emphasizing these refinements? Why are you at such pains to assure us that the Dutch have taken Holland?" Undoubtedly, it is a theoretical and a sufficiently obvious distinction to which we call attention here ; nevertheless, many detractors of political economy have overlooked this distinction ; and a large part of the criticisms of economics lose all their force when confronted with the right understanding of the province of the science. In fact, misconception of this province brings political economy into disrepute in two ways—(a) by causing people to expect impossible things from the science, (*b*) by alienating a class of people to whom it is especially important that political economy should not be repugnant.

First, we say, this failure to recognize the proper office of economics imposes upon the science, already staggering under its burdens, graver responsibilities than any science can assume. Political economy, according to one view, must either show that whatever is, is right; or must at once make right whatever is wrong. Mr. Ruskin upbraids political economy for not preventing strikes; but what has political economy to do with preventing strikes? Just as reasonably might one abuse astronomy for not preventing shipwrecks, or hold chemistry accountable for dynamite explosions. In the same way Mr. H. D. Lloyd speaks[1] of political economy as "the science that claims to be able to reconcile self-interest with the harmony of interests." Some students of political economy—notably Carey and Bastiat—have advanced some such utopian view of the

[1] *Atlantic Monthly*, v. 50, p. 70.

universe; but the science of political economy could not becomingly make such pretensions—in fact, could not "claim" any thing except a single-hearted purpose to discover truth.

The second serious consequence of misinterpreting the aim of economics—estranging from the study the laboring classes—has been pointed out[1] by Professor Cairnes: "Political economy too often makes its appearance, especially in its approaches to the working classes, in the guise of a dogmatic code of cut-and-dried rules. . . . Now when we take into account the sort of decrees which are ordinarily given to the world in the name of Political Economy—decrees which, I think I may say in the main amount to a handsome ratification of the existing form of society as approximately perfect—I think we shall be able to understand the repugnance, and even violent opposition, manifested towards it by people who have their own reasons for not cherishing that unbounded admiration for our present in-

[1] "Logical Method," pp. 25, 26.

dustrial arrangements which is felt by some popular expositors of so-called economic laws. When a working man is told that Political Economy 'condemns' strikes, hesitates about co-operation, looks askance at proposals for limiting the hours of labor, but 'approves' the accumulation of capital, and 'sanctions' the market rate of wages, it seems not an unnatural response that 'since Political Economy is against the working man, it behooves the working man to be against Political Economy.'" What wonder is it that, under these conditions, the working man fears political economy even when it brings him priceless gifts? The truth is, of course, that political economy merely asserts that certain effects follow certain causes, without predicating any thing whatever as to the character of those effects, whether they be good or bad; and it is equally a matter of course that political economy does not "condemn" one thing any more than it "approves" another. Chemistry tells us what effect follows the introduction into the human system of a *quantum sufficit* of prussic acid; and may be said, in a certain sense, to "condemn" the personal application of that acid; it is only in a similar sense that political economy can be said to condemn any thing.

This conception of economics as a science, with the necessary limitations of a science, is no doubt disappointing to the ambition of some economists; but such a conception is required by the nature of the study; and, moreover, whatever the science loses in the grandeur of its aim will be more than made up in the number and greater value of its achievements. Only by thus narrowing the field can we hope, with Mr. Bagehot, to show that "political economy is not a questionable thing of unlimited extent, but a most certain and useful thing of limited extent." [1] We shall have to recur to this subject at a later stage of our discussion, in connection with the doctrines of the new school of economic writers: the point that we would emphasize here is, that the present unsatisfactory condition of economics, as regards

[1] "Economic Studies," p. 21.

popular favor, is traceable in part to a general misunderstanding of the real province of the science.

A second reason for the ill-repute that attaches to economics at present may be found in the seemingly chaotic condition in which the science is left by its ever-discordant expounders. Probably Mr. Cairnes is right in saying [1] that if we include all economic writers—sciolists as well as men of established reputation,—there is not a single doctrine of the science that is undisputed. Of course, a large part of these dissentients may be dismissed with the same mild compassion that we bestow upon the occasional "crank" (what other word will do?), who stakes his fortune on the flatness of the earth. Still, a considerable body of authoritative writers disagree, or, at any rate, seem to disagree, on cardinal points in the science. A somewhat emphatic but fairly typical example of this is afforded by one phase of the famous wages-

[1] "Logical Method," p. 219.

fund controversy—a controversy so aptly illustrative of what we said about economic disputants, and so delightfully diverting withal, that we cannot forbear a brief description.

Economist A. propounds a theory of wages, which is generally accepted, and becomes a part of all the books on the subject. After many years economist B. attacks this doctrine by asking a series of questions on the points involved, or supposed to be involved, in the theory. "It sounds like mockery or childishness to ask these questions," says B., "so obvious are the only answers that can possibly be given to them; yet it is only on the assumption that directly opposite answers must be given that the wages fund can for one moment stand." Now, economist A. has long since put away childish things, and, admitting the pertinency of these questions, he surrenders at discretion. If the blind lead the blind, both shall fall into the ditch, thinks economist C., who now steps into the arena to take up the cudgels against both A. and B.

C. is lost in wonder at the alacrity with which A. beat a retreat, and he cannot believe his senses when he finds him accepting B.'s series of questions as involving a fair statement of the wages-fund theory. C. would have "confidently asserted, he will not say that no economist, but that no reasonable being had ever advanced the theory of a wages fund in that sense." A charitable world has commonly regarded John Stuart Mill as a "reasonable being," and would probably place Mr. Cairnes and Mr. Thornton in the same exalted category. Nevertheless, each of the three solutions of this economic problem presented by these three reasonable men seems to one of those men eminently rational, and to the other two grotesquely absurd. Episodes of this kind are not without a certain interest, especially from a psychological point of view; but they hardly redound to the credit of political economy, as they certainly do not inspire confidence in economists.

But the case might be worse; the presumption against economics, arising from the lack of harmony among economic writers, is not so strong as might at first appear. A very large proportion of the unnumbered economic controversies would fall into one of the three following classes : (*a*) Many controversies relate rather to form than to substance, and are, after all, of minor importance. Gallons of good ink and tons of excellent paper have been consumed to no better purpose than " doting about questions and the strifes of words," —mere matters of definition. Whether or not the term wealth should include mental qualities and acquired skill, whether or not actors and musicians should be classed as productive laborers—these and many other questions of nomenclature are interesting enough in their way, and are not without a certain importance ; but the existence of such questions does not argue a serious imperfection in the science. (*b*) Many supposed issues would be found, if the disputants understood each other, to belong to what Professor Simon Newcomb calls [1] "that large and alluring class of

[1] " Principles of Political Economy," preface.

questions in which there is no point at issue." In economics, as in other departments of knowledge, infinite trouble arises, because " some people will not take the trouble to understand what other people say." (*c*) By far the larger part of the so-called economic controversies relate, not to the science itself, but to its applications ; and such contentions, as we have tried to show in preceding pages, are not, properly speaking. economic controversies at all.

A very large proportion of the disputes in economics would be included, as we have said, in the foregoing classes ; and their existence, accordingly, would not constitute a very formidable indictment against political economy. But it cannot be denied—and it ought, perhaps, to be pointed out here—that another set of controversies are far more dangerous to the good repute of economics, and call in question the very foundation upon which the science rests. It would take us too far afield to attempt an adequate defence of this condition of things—not to mention the trifling circumstance that the task is altogether beyond our powers. Still, sometimes a Davus can suggest a plan that only an Œdipus can execute. As regards most of these fundamental controversies, both statements of the case seem reasonable; and, where this is so, perhaps our wisest course will be, not to insist upon a single view of the question, but to search for some common ground upon which diverse opinions may be compromised and reconciled.

Take, for example, the wages-fund controversy—a fundamental question and yet one upon which economists seem to be hopelessly divided. That the wages of labor are causally connected in some way with the product of labor, seems not to require argument, and General Walker's theory of wages, of which this proposition is the gist, seems, accordingly, incapable of refutation. When, however, we turn to that *facile princeps* of recent economists, Professor J. E. Cairnes, we find another theory of wages, consisting of a chain of reasoning of which the several links are so firmly bound together that the best equipped logician cannot hope to tear them asunder. Must we, then, in the face of these two rival theories, admit that this important block in the economic groundwork is insecure? There are two avenues of escape from this conclusion—(*a*) by showing that one of the theories is logically at fault; (*b*) by showing that one of the theories includes the other, or that the two are reconcilable.

The former of these conceivable ways out of the difficulty is closed to us, since both theories seem to be logically without a flaw; but the other loophole remains, and, in fact, is sufficient for our purposes. For why are the two theories incompatible? General Walker's chapter on the wages question[1] has commonly been regarded as laying down new views; but it seems sufficiently clear that Mill and his school recognized the part that the product plays in determining wages. The production of a series of years determines (conjointly with other things) the amount

[1] "Wages Question," chap. ix.

of capital that will be in existence at the end of these years : and at this point Professor Cairnes's theory comes in to determine the rate of wages. The two theories view the situation from somewhat different standpoints, and serve somewhat different purposes ; but the theories are not mutually exclusive, and the economic substructure is rather strengthened than weakened by these complemental doctrines.

What is true of the controversy as to wages is probably true in the case of other fundamental questions, namely, that opposing views may be reconciled and shown to be essentially consistent. As regards the question with which we are immediately concerned—that of economic methods—we shall find something distinctly like this to be the case.

In my endeavor satisfactorily to account for the present disrepute of economics, I must not forget a circumstance that will readily suggest itself to any one familiar with economic discussions, namely, the startling incompetence of many critics of political economy. Mill deems it an advantage that the nomenclature of economics is made up of words in common use : and undoubtedly this would be an advantage, if these common words had their common meanings. But the fact is, that the most important terms in economics—for example, rent, capital, distribution, cost of production — have meanings strictly technical, and frequently quite unlike the common meaning ; so that the advantage in this nomenclature is, after all, rather dubious. Tell the average untaught man some marvel of astronomy—that Arcturus travels fifty-four miles a second, or that the North-star, for aught we know to the contrary, may have been annihilated forty-eight years ago, and he will listen in large-eyed wonder, and will never dream of disputing your statement. But tell the same man some economic commonplace—that the millions of dollars paid every year in rent has no effect on the price of bread, or that high wages indicate low cost of production : and this time, too, he will listen in wide-mouthed astonishment—astonishment at your "plentiful lack of wit."

Cost of production is a familiar phrase to him, and your statement will cause him to look at you suspiciously, to tap his forehead significantly, and, finally, to direct you to the nearest lunatic asylum.

So it is in many cases. The technical terms of economics are familiar to every one; and every one, consequently, feels competent to sound the depths of any economic question. If the bare-footed philosopher of Athens could walk our streets to-day, he would find, in the discussions of economics, abundant opportunities for enjoying his favorite pastime—exposing "the conceit of knowledge without the reality." No one, without having first made some study of the subject, would presume to give an opinion upon a nice point of chemical analysis; nor would any one attempt to discuss off-hand the theorem of homogeneous functions or the subtilties of the solar parallax: but every man you meet can tell you all about taxation and finance, even though he has never opened an economic text-book. In these days of learned blacksmiths and geologist stonemasons one has to be very careful about warning shoe-makers not to go beyond their lasts: but perhaps the ancient adage might be aptly quoted at times to our curbstone economists. "It would be too much to expect," says one writer, in the bitterness of his heart, "that those who attack political economy should make a serious effort to know any thing about it."

Political economy has gained nothing before the world from a wide-spread notion that economic doctrines are tinged or, rather, deeply dyed with the darkest kind of gloom. It was Carlyle, we believe, who first called economics "the dismal science": but the world quickly caught up this *lucus a non lucendo*, feeling assured that political economy had come into being only to answer in the affirmative the poet's question,

> "O Star-eyed Science! hast thou wandered there
> To waft us home the message of despair?"

Mr. Rickards of Oxford declared[1] thirty years ago that political economy charged

---

[1] "Population and Capital," preface.

the Creator with having made a " miscalculation of means to ends in the arrangements of the universe " : and the latest attempt to raze the economic structure to the ground—that of Mr. Henry George—emphasizes this count in the general indictment against political economy.

The first thing to be said about this view of economics is, that it has a certain foundation in fact : and the next thing to be said is, that this foundation is very unsubstantial, and is quite incapable of supporting any serious charge against the science. In the first place, one may well ask how far, in a world so badly put together as ours, apparent resulting harmoies can be accepted as establishing the truth of an economic proposition. Certainly, Bastiat's example will not inspire confidence in the accuracy of this test: since, in his case, we have a "set of harmonies which, it seems to be agreed on all sides, are admirable in every respect except consonance with fact."[1] There is no doubt, I suppose, that much of Henry

[1] C. F. Dunbar, *Quarterly Journal of Economics*, No. 1.

C. Carey's extraordinary popularity is due to the harmonious and optimistic nature of his doctrines: but it is difficult to make out the economic grounds on which he based his rose-colored views of the universe.[1]

I admitted, just now, some slight foundation for the popular notion that identifies

---

[1] In the preface to "Social Science" Carey lays claim to three great discoveries, of which the first and second are, respectively, a theory of value embracing all kinds of products, and the idea of a certain kind of distribution between capital and labor, by which capital gets a continually decreasing, and labor a continually increasing, proportion of the return. Then Carey goes on to say that the "third and fundamental law remained to be discovered and may be found in the second chapter of the present volume." Diligent search in that chapter will not bring to light any "great law." Perhaps Mr. Carey referred to what is contained in a paragraph on the thirty-seventh page. "We have here the great law of Molecular Gravitation," etc. He seems to think that there is a social law of gravitation analogous to that of the physical world. Most readers, however, would regard his language as nothing more than an injudicious use of metaphor to illustrate the flights of a daring imagination. It is worth while to note the fact that Carey's followers have not in all cases trodden in the steps of their master. Professor Robert E. Thompson, for example, accepts the law of value and the anti-Ricardian law, but is not so certain of the resulting harmony; and he has nothing to say about the elusive law for which we have just been searching—the "law of Social Gravitation."

economics with the Slough of Despond: and it cannot be denied that some of the earlier economists could hardly have furnished much inspiration for a Miltonic "L'Allegro." Malthus, for example, declares[1]: "If my views are adopted, we shall be compelled to acknowledge that the poverty and misery which prevail among the lower classes are absolutely irremediable." Elsewhere Malthus cheers on sanitary commissioners with this confident assertion: "I feel not the slightest doubt that if the introduction of the cow-pox should extirpate the small-pox and yet the number of marriages continue the same, we should find a very perceptible difference in the increased mortality of some other disease." In 1819, Sismondi published his "New Principles of Political Economy," their chief claim to novelty residing in the high-pitched tone of despair with which they discussed all things human. The industrial machinery of the

[1] Preface, first edition of the essay on population. It should be said that in subsequent editions this view was somewhat modified; Malthus was able to "soften some of the harshest conclusions."

world seemed to Sismondi to have been thrown permanently out of gear: and, though he advocated some extraordinary remedies, of which economics is not proud, he still felt obliged to admit that the case was utterly hopeless.

When political economy presents itself in such an attitude as this—when leading economists can find no better occupation than "folding their arms and leaving the *dénouement* to time and Providence"—it is not surprising that "economists" and "pessimists" should become in the popular vocabulary convertible terms. Nevertheless, the answer to all this is not far to seek, and is found in the proper conception of economics. When we remember that political economy consists of deductions and inductions, of series of syllogisms and chains of reasoning, of a body of logical processes leading up to and establishing certain irrevocable laws—laws in the sense of the Newtonian laws of motion or the law of gravitation,—when we remember this, we see at once that such an epithet as "dismal" is not applicable to political economy. What should we think of the man who should say, "The tenth proposition of Euclid has always seemed to me shamefully hard-hearted"; or of the man who, because railroad accidents sometimes occur, should call mechanics a "peculiarly inhuman science"? If such qualities were predicable of a science, economics might more truly be described as *benevolent*, since it contemplates, through its applications, better and better conditions of human existence.

Another source of the present deep-seated prejudice against political economy may be found in the circumstance that men's personal interests are directly involved in the science. The cynical Hobbes declared that the axioms of geometry would be disputed, if men's passions were implicated therein; and Archbishop Whately, with an equally exact knowledge of human frailties, said that the demonstrations of Euclid would not have commanded universal assent if they had been applicable to the pursuits of individuals. That the Bessemer steel manufacturers, or the Nevada silver kings, or the extreme socialists, should receive political economy with open arms and proclaim its merits from the housetops, is not to be expected at this distance from the millennium : and even that the more numerous class of people, whose immediate interests are less closely connected with economic doctrines, and who merely find the truths of economics somewhat unwelcome—that such persons should be loud in their praises of political economy, is not in the course of human nature. Still, it is not a philosophic procedure to call a science names because it brings to light disagreeable truths. Besides, there is little to be gained by railing at the tranquil facts of the universe : "The only argument available with the east wind," says Lowell, "is to put on your overcoat."

A final cause of this extensive disaffection with economic science—a more deep-reaching cause, perhaps, than some of those hitherto noticed—is to be sought in the mistakes of the expounders of that science. Bastiat's famous conceit of the chandlers' and lamp-manufacturers' petition for the exclusion of the light of the sun has its counterpart in some of the doctrines actually promulgated at different times by economists. Madame de Staël said that she was sorry to hear that a man had made a good bargain, because she knew that the other man had made a bad bargain; and she might have pleaded, in defence of this view, the authority of one of England's greatest economists before Adam Smith: for Sir James Stuart used the same reasoning in the case of international trade, declaring that, "if one country gains, another must lose."[1] That a pound of lead is no heavier than a pound of feathers,[2] is known in every kinder-garten: but a whole school of economists once taught that a dollar's worth of gold was worth more than a dollar's worth of any thing else; and the policy of great

[1] "Inquiries into the Principles of Political Economy" (1767). Compare Voltaire: "Such is the condition of humanity that to wish the greatness of one's own country, is to wish evil to one's neighbors. It is clear that one country cannot gain unless another loses."

[2] Henry George uses this illustration for a similar purpose.

nations was shaped on this assumption. One of the ablest of French economists deprecated the use of machinery, and advised the government to discourage inventions by refusing to grant patents.[1]

These and many other economical the-

[1] These very unorthodox products of political economy, brought to maturity by Sismondi, will appear less exotic, if we recall the circumstances under which they grew up. The decade immediately succeeding the Napoleonic wars forms, in the industrial history of the world, an epoch of which the counterpart cannot easily be found. The commercial world found itself, after the wars of the French Revolution, in a most abnormal condition—a great transformation of industry due to English inventions, the shock to existing arrangements implied in the transition from war to peace, the changed conditions under which division of labor was to be resumed ; and all complicated by a progressive fall of prices due to improved processes and by tariff changes in the case of leading countries. There is only one way of describing such a condition of things—it was a time of adjustment between supply and demand, a period of transition from one industrial age to another. So strong a case for the theory of a general overproduction was never presented before, and probably will never again arise. We need not wonder, then, that Sismondi, living in the midst of the movement and therefore viewing it with no perspective, allowed the things that were seen to blind his eyes to other discernible things. Mr. Edward Atkinson is anxious to examine the " outside of the head of any one who pleads a general over-production, in order to see how his brain is constituted, and what element of commonsense has been omitted in his make-up." But even commonsense is not enough in the case of some economic problems : there must be added a very uncommon discretion.

ories of the past may be classed with the "Portuguese Phrase-Book," as "jest in sober earnest": but even the current economic doctrines, though not so ludicrously erroneous as some of their predecessors, are yet far from invulnerable. Economists sometimes draw their inferences prematurely; they are prone to push doctrines too far, to state conclusions in too absolute a form; and they frequently fail to notice disturbing elements, thereby making their principles unduly inelastic. Of course, all this is saying only that economists are men: still, the effect of such mistakes on the reputation of economics is none the less marked; and perhaps to this cause—the shortcomings of economists—as much as to any other, is due the present disrepute of political economy.

By the foregoing exposition of what we conceive to be causes adequately and satisfactorily explaining the stigma that rests upon economic studies, we have cleared the way, perhaps, for the second part of our subject—"the demand for a radical change" in the methods and aims of political economy. That demand, as our glance at the present condition of economics showed only too well, is imperative and persistent, and deserves attention not less from the authoritative character of the makers than from their number. The first sign of revolt appeared in Germany, in Wilhelm Roscher's writings, so far back as 1843 [1] : and throughout the contest the Germans, with their characteristic *penchant* for contention, have been foremost in stirring up mutiny in the economic camp. Partly from this circumstance the new school has sometimes been called the "German" school: but the movement soon outgrew this name. Equally insufficient is the epithet "Realistic," though it serves the useful purpose of covertly reproving the alleged abstract character of the "Orthodox" economics. No one who has the interest of the new school at heart will admit the adequacy of the term "Inductive." The word "Historical" is, perhaps, most suggestive of the real character of the new movement.

[1] "Grundriss zu Vorlesungen über die Staatswirthschaft nach geschichtlicher Methode."

IV.

GENERAL STATEMENT OF THE ENGLISH METHOD IN ECONOMICS.

The careful and complete exposition of the methods of the English school, given by Professor Cairnes in his "Logical Method of Political Economy," ought to prevent any misapprehension as to what that school professes to do. The fact, however, that misapprehension exists, is clearly shown by the nature of the objections made to the old school. Before attempting, therefore, to expound the doctrines of the new school I must in self-defence trace out roughly the general lines upon which the "Orthodox" economists develop their science.

In fact, the method of the English economists is extremely simple. Starting with certain mental principles, so manifest that statement and demonstration are one, and adding to these certain physical conditions, less obvious than the mental principles but equally beyond dispute, the economist finds in these premises a sound basis for deductive reasoning. These few premises, embodying the leading causes in the production and the distribution of wealth, form the groundwork upon which all economic science must, according to the English school, be established. It is not, however, supposed that this foundation alone is sufficient to support the vast superstructure of political economy. The complexity of human nature is so great, and the facts to be taken account of are so numerous, that we cannot hope to formulate all the causes affecting the phenomena of wealth. The most that we can do is to lay down these broad and universal truths, and to incorporate among them, as the science grows, such other subordinate influences as are seen to be effective economic motors.

The laws of political economy are, for the most part, inferences from these general facts: and, if there were not numerous exceptional cases and modifying circumstances, the maxims of the science, as Professor Francis Bowen says,[1] might be taken for granted, and political economy might be called an intuitive or even a demonstrative science. But man is a many-impulsed creature, and the economist has constant need to remember the logician's warning that "there is a false simplicity about analysis, a standing failure in all attempts to cram the universe into labelled nut-shells." What befalls the economist who forgets this has been happily illustrated by Mr. Ruskin : " We have made learned experiments upon pure nitrogen, and have convinced ourselves that it is a very manageable gas ; but behold ! the thing which we have practically to deal with is its chloride, and this, the moment we touch it on our established principles, sends us with our apparatus through the ceiling." Disturbing causes in economics frequently enough have this chemcal nature : and the economist is obliged at every step to test his conclusions reach-

[1] "American Political Economy," p. 131 (ed. of 1859).

ed by deductive reasoning with the actual course of affairs in the economic world : that is to say, induction corrects and supplements deduction in the logical method of the English school.

According to Cliffe Leslie,[1] there are two systems of economics descended from Adam Smith, of which one combines the *a priori* and the inductive methods in the way that I have just described. But Mr. Leslie speaks of another system," of which Mr. Ricardo was the founder, reasoning entirely from hypothetical laws or principles of nature, and discarding induction, not only for the ascertainment of its premises, but even for the verification of its deductive conclusions."[2] I must admit that I never before heard of this latter school ; and my browsings among economic books have never discovered any products of such a school, —a regrettable fact, since economic literature with such a foundation could not fail to be highly entertaining. Without challenging Mr. Leslie's statement more dis-

---

[1] " Essays on Political and Moral Philosophy," p. 151.
[2] " Essays," etc., p. 151.

Economical Science. 47

tinctly, it is sufficient here to say that the method described by him is certainly not the English method—at least, if we may allow English economists to define their own method. That method, as we have seen, uses deduction and induction alternately, and accounts the verification and correction of conclusions by the inductive tests of experience no less important than the forming of conclusions by deductive reasoning.

One economist, impatient of certain misconceptions of his views, declared, with that delicate regard for others' feelings so characteristic of economic writers, that he "could find his opponents in arguments, but not in brains": without hinting at the possibility of any personal application, I may yet be pardoned, perhaps, for quoting this Johnsonian reminiscence in connection with the palpable misconceptions of "Orthodox" doctrines sometimes shown by critics of those doctrines. It is not a flattering commentary upon human credulity that some people really seem to think that the English economists start with a single assumption—men desire wealth—and build up the whole science on that alone. "In abstract political economy," says [1] Mr. H. D. Lloyd, "wealth is the subject, desire of wealth the motive, competition the regulator, supply and demand the law, freedom of contract the condition, and equalization of rent, wages, other prices, and profits the result." Yes, but every "abstract" economist knows that "desire of wealth" is frequently not the only motive; that competition is sometimes wanting, and therefore cannot "regulate"; that supply and demand is not "*the* law," but *a* law; that the condition of "freedom of contract" is often not realized; and that in all these cases the "result" will be affected accordingly.

One of the most notable contributions to economics in recent years is Mr. J. K. Ingram's article on political economy in the last edition of the "Encyclopædia Britannica"; and yet it would seem as if —let us euphemize and call it inadequacy of statement—could not further go than

[1] *Atlantic Monthly*, vol. l., p. 73.

in the following characterization of English economics: " The value of most of the theorems of the classical economics is a good deal attenuated by the habitual assumption that we are dealing with 'economic men,' actuated by one principle only ; that custom, as against competition, has no existence ; that there is no such thing as combination ; that there is equality of contract between the parties to each transaction, and that there is a defined universal rate of profit and wages in a community, which implies that the capital embarked in any undertaking will pass at once to another in which larger profits are for the time to be made ; that a laborer, whatever his local ties of feeling, family, habit, or other engagements, will transfer himself immediately to any place where, or employment in which, for the time, larger wages are to be earned than those he had previously obtained ; and that both capitalists and laborers have a perfect knowledge of the condition and the prospects of industry throughout the country, both in their own and other occupations."[1] If other parts of Mr. Ingram's treatise did not show minute acquaintance with " Orthodox " writings, one could hardly withhold the belief that Mr. Ingram's fondness for German economics had led him to neglect all that has been written in England on the subject in the last half century. Chapters, essays, whole volumes, indeed, have been written by English economists to prove the invalidity of these doctrines, and to point out the limitations with which such doctrines must be received : there is hardly one of the " habitual assumptions " ascribed by Mr. Ingram to the classical economics that, in the sense in which he seems to understand them, has not been repudiated time and again and with all possible emphasis by English economists.

Having now glanced at the method of the " Orthodox " economists, and having seen in that way the need of caution in taking at second hand the doctrines of the

[1] " Encycl. Britannica," ninth edition, vol. xix., p. 375.

English school, we are prepared more intelligently to discuss the merits of proposed substitutes. Some difficulty arises at the outset from the circumstance that not all historical economists are agreed as to the precise character of the new doctrines: not only is the economic house divided against itself, but even the resulting sections must needs be subdivided. On one point, to be sure, historical writers agree wonderfully well—that is, in crying down the old economics and proclaiming the necessity of a radical change ; but when the exact nature of that change is defined, the standards clash again. Indeed, the spirit of the new school seems to be rather negative than positive, rather iconoclastic than constructive. The German and especially the English adherents of the new school, have devoted more time to the finding of weak points in the old system than to the establishment of sound principles in the new. Accordingly, we can, perhaps, best begin our exposition of the Historical school by considering their criticisms of the older economics.

V.

THE NEGATIVE SIDE OF THE NEW SCHOOL.

One of the stock arguments against the " abstract " political economy—that it is exclusively deductive, and thus deals with theories rather than with facts—has already been disposed of in our statement of the English scientific method. This criticism is urged with great fervor by the new school; but the attitude of that school, as regards the proper sphere of deduction in economic inquiry, is by no means fixed. In Germany some of the more extreme Historical writers—Schmoller and his school—allow deduction no place in their economic method: on the ground, presumably, that deduction is not required in the mere observation and registration of economic events. The founders of the German school did not so lightly cast aside deduction, seeing with

Economical Science.

Professor Cairnes that one might reason inductively "till the crack of doom without arriving at any conclusion of the slightest value."[1] So, too, Wagner and other contemporary economists in Germany protest against the purely inductive method, affirming that economists are something more than mere annalists, and that economic theory is a thing quite distinct from economic history.[2]

The English Historical economists apparently do not quite agree with either

[1] "Logical Method," p. 65.
[2] There is a course of study in Harvard College—Political Economy IV. or, "The economic history of Europe and America since the Seven Years' war"—that stands on the border-line between political economy and history, and that illustrates well the difference between economic history and economic theory. This course traces the economic effects of those great industrial and political movements that have so profoundly influenced, in the last 125 years, the production and the distribution of wealth—the invention of textile machinery, the applications of steam, the American and French Revolutions, the new discoveries of gold, the civil war of '61-5, the political reorganization of Germany, and so forth. Some of these subjects can be fully understood only by a person familiar with economic science; in the main, however, the study is historical, and economic history is so far divorced from economic theory that the course is open to students who have made no previous study of political economy.

branch of their German colleagues. Cliffe Leslie devoted an essay[1] to the elaboration of the thesis that the "economic world is an unknown world," and that, accordingly, political economy has not yet reached, in its scientific development, the deductive stage. Mr. Ingram, also, looks askance at deduction, declaring that we cannot "assume as universal premises the convenient formulas that have been habitually employed, such as that all men desire wealth." In his view, however, the economic world is not so completely unknown as to exclude all use of deduction, since he adds: "Whilst eliminating all premature assumptions, we shall use the ascertained truths respecting human nature as guides in the inquiry and aids toward the interpretation of facts."[2] This resolve commands an easy approval: and why are not those "convenient formulas habitually employed" just such "ascertained truths respecting human nature"? If the assumption that all men desire

[1] *Fortnightly Review*, vol. xxxi., p. 934.
[2] "Encycl. Britan.," etc., p. 400.

Economical Science. 55

wealth is "premature," we may hope that all future premises of the science will be equally precocious in developing.

Thus, when our historical critics ring the various changes of this "exclusively-deductive" argument, the impulse is irresistible to make a casual remark about people who live in glass houses; but the English school need not resort to the *tu quoque* argument. The fact is, that the English method, so far from being exclusively deductive, is constantly and necessarily inductive, and is avowedly crude and wholly insufficient without that attribute. Such is the theory; and the practice of leading English economists has been in perfect accord with the theory. As for Adam Smith, Hildebrand and other Historical authors claim him for their own; and whoever has turned the fact-laden pages of the "Wealth of Nations" will never charge the Scotch professor with having favored unduly any one logical process. Malthus's work was about five parts historic to one part economic, and induction was summoned at every step to clinch the deductive argument. At the present time, surely, Wall Street and the Bourse do not predispose men to favor theorizing, and probably in Ricardo's day the Stock Exchange tended just as little to make men "dreamers of dreams and spinners of abstract fancies."[1] Without going through the chapter we may say, generally, that the English economists have followed the example set by their Scotch progenitor, and have ever regarded a theory inadequately supported by facts as a much worse predicament than facts uninterpreted by a theory. When Mr.

[1] Still, Ricardo, though a successful man of business, and thus not likely to be over-fond of abstract speculation, has probably more than any other English economist provoked this charge against the "Orthodox" economics of undue attention to theories. Ricardo's method is severely scientific; the reasoning is close, and much is left for the reader to get between the lines. Ricardo himself averred that not more than five and twenty persons understood his book; and even his translators are not to be included in that chosen circle. Bagehot speaks of the "anxious penetration with which Ricardo follows out rarefied minutiæ," and even this highly charged statement does not adequately describe the Ricardian tendency to subtilize. Even so, Jevons goes too far in saying that Ricardo shunted the car of economic science on to the wrong track; at any rate, Mill and Cairnes have switched the car back again.

Bagehot calls the German method in disparagement an "all-case" method, Mr. Leslie retorts that a "no-case" method is worse. This rejoinder is more remarkable for its truth than for its pertinency, since the English method is far from a "no-case" method, and would be aptly described (if we may torture the mother-tongue a little more) as the "enough-case" method. "Rapidity and daring in deduction," says Ingram, "may be the greatest of dangers, if they are divorced from a wide and balanced appreciation of facts": the method of the English economists contemplates the use of a sufficient number of cases to prevent any such separation of fact and theory.

Among the shortcomings of economists we noticed[1] a tendency to "state their conclusions in too absolute a form"—to conceive of their principles as universal and immutable truths : and this tendency has been magnified into a positive transgression by the economists of the new school. At the Adam Smith centenary

[1] *Ante*, p. 41.

dinner, before referred to in these pages, Mr. Lowe (now Lord Sherbrooke) made a somewhat unfortunate remark to the effect that political economy had about finished its work. This remark was simply pounced upon by the Historical economists, and has been rolled under their tongues ever since as a sweet morsel for criticism. We shall see later how much political economy has still before itself: and we mention this incident here only as a marked example of the tendency to regard the teachings of economics as truths for all time. Whether or not all things, as the old Greek philosopher declared, are relative, it is certain that some of the theories and very many of the applications of political economy are strictly contingent. From the way in which the economists of the new school have accentuated this truth one might suppose that the discovery was original with them. They are constantly assuring us, with the emphasis and the iteration appropriate to the exposition of a great scientific achievement, that economics is not a body of changeless laws—nay, according to some historical authors, is not a body of laws at all.[1] The conclusions of former economists (continue the critics) may have been valid when first drawn, but such conclusions are useless for the practical purposes of the statesmen of to-day. Each nation, as well as each epoch, has its own political economy quite distinct from that of every other nation and every other age.

This is what the critics say; and, strangely enough, this is what the criticised say, also: only the latter do not say it so loudly, and do not think the statement of such importance that they must needs have it for preface, and text, and appendix. Still,

[1] " Political economy is not a body of natural laws, . . . but an assemblage of speculations and doctrines " (Cliffe Leslie, " Essays in Political and Moral Philosophy," p. 148). Dr. Edwin Seligman, also, reproaches the English school for the " pretence of having discovered economic laws." This offence would seem not to include all the crimes in the decalogue, and probably the English writers would not hesitate to own the soft impeachment. At any rate they sin in good company, since Mr. Ingram criticises the German school for denying the existence of economic laws. For an admirable statement of the sense in which there are economic laws, see Ingram, " Encyc. Br.," etc., p. 392. Cf. Cairnes, " Essays in Political Economy, Theoretical and Applied," pp. 254, 255.

English economists have not deceived themselves in this respect; they have recognized the limitations of their subject, and have been glad to believe that their science is infinitely perfectible. Before taking up the subject of distribution, Mill notices[1] the fact that the laws and the conditions of that subject differ from those of the production of wealth in being more arbitrary, and, therefore, less general. The laws of the production of wealth (he says) are like physical truths, having nothing optional in them; but the distribution of wealth is a matter of human institution solely. Depending thus on the laws and customs of society, the principles underlying the distribution of wealth will vary as laws and customs vary. In the same way Mr. Bagehot devotes an essay to pointing out the limitations of economic truths, and declares that economics is only a " convenient series of deductions from assumed axioms which are never quite true, which in many times and countries would be

[1] " Principles of Political Economy " (Laughlin's edition), p. 155.

utterly untrue, but which are sufficiently near to the conditions of the modern world to make it useful to consider them by themselves."

In taking this view of their subject, the English economists have done only what was strictly required by the nature of their logical method. So far as altered political conditions, or new industrial systems, or improved productive processes, or shifting social relations, or any thing else affects the production and the distribution of wealth, so far must the science be recast by the insertion of new data and the correction—perhaps the abandonment —of old premises : and so far forth will the economist regard his conclusions as provisional and his laws as transitory ; to this extent he will distrust the teachings of the past, and will agree with Dr. Ely that the " political economy of to-day is not that of to-morrow." In one way, indeed, economics is the very Penelope of sciences, plying its tasks over and over again, as the march of human affairs undoes the work of the past.

But we must not attach too great importance to this aspect of political economy. Mr. Cairnes somewhat impatiently asks,[1] "Will people never understand that a 'law' of political economy is a 'law' in no other sense than the law of gravitation?" And, in fact, so long as the premises from which the economist reasons are true, so long must the logical conclusion follow as immutably as the sequence of cause and effect in the case of any purely physical law. Morever, the differences in the relative importance of the premises of the science are, for the most part, rather theoretical than actual. No one can dispute Dr. Seligman's assertion that the explanations of phenomena are inextricably interwoven with the institutions of the period: but the great "institutions of the period"—private property, capital, credit, the relation of employer and employee, and so on—are the same the world over. It is conceivable, of course, that these economic arrangements of mankind may change; that the institution of private property may

[1] "Leading Principles," p. 111.

Economical Science. 63

give way to a communistic *régime ;* that the relation of employer and employee may be replaced by a system of co-operative industry. But these, after all, are remote contingencies, and do not much affect the practical question. The great and fundamental laws of economics are essentially the same for all the countries and all the times with which economists are concerned : and in these days of ever-improving communications, when local peculiarities are fast fading away, even the less important principles of the science will not need essential modification in different places. In short, both the fundamental and the incidental premises of economics are, and can hardly fail to remain, cosmopolitan : " There is no more a French or German or American political economy or political science than there is a German or French or American science of astronomy or chemistry."[1]

"Only through the principle of competition has political economy any preten-

[1] Lalor's "Cyclopædia of Political Science," preface.

sion to the character of a science," says[1] Mill; and English economists in general have regarded competition as bearing to their science the same fundamental relation that, for example, the law of gravitation bears to the science of astronomy. Historical economists, however, attach less importance to this factor of industry, and declare that many flaws in the current doctrines are due to an exclusive dependence upon competition as the solvent in which all economic problems may be resolved. Competition (runs the criticism) is of the first importance to the economist; but it cannot, by itself, explain some of the most striking phenomena of industrial life; "by neglecting the other forces [ranging] from sympathy to monopoly, the abstract political economist deduces principles that fit no realities, and has to neglect those realities for which we need principles most. When combination comes in at the door, this political economy of competition flies out of the window."[2]

[1] "Principles of Political Economy" (Laughlin's edit.), p. 175.
[2] *Atlantic Monthly*, vol. l., p. 75 (H. D. Lloyd).

In these days of millionaires and multi-millionaires combination frequently does cross the threshold ; and in this emergency "the political economy of competition" cannot do better than take itself off at short notice : but the English political economy, if true to its logical method, will not remain, under these conditions, a political economy of competition. Historical economists may well emphasize the modern drift toward an era of custom and combination. Unquestionably, the current of industrial life to-day sets strongly in this direction. Now, more than when "Locksley Hall" was written, does "the individual wither." On every side giant monopolies, trade coalitions, and industrial leagues of all kinds have come into being : and the inquiries, how far this movement is a legitimate and useful reorganization, making more effective, as parts of a general system, detached and inefficient industrial bodies ; and how far, on the other hand, the movement is unlawful as violating the rights of consumers,—these are questions that call for the nicest discrimination on the part of economist and statesman. So far as Historical writers address themselves to these questions, or sound the note of alarm, so far they acquit themselves well, and make no mistake. But it is a mistake to suppose that this state of things is beyond the reach of the English economics: this is just the contingency contemplated by Mr. Cairnes, when he says[1]: "Many subordinate influences will intervene to disturb, and occasionally to reverse, the operation of the more powerful principles." It is obvious that the effect of monopoly will be to make void any deductions that derive their cogency from the supposed existence of competition. In the presence of this new power political economy must recast its premises, and adapt itself to the changed conditions.

This is required by the logical method of the English economics; and this is, in fact, what leading English economists have done. One hundred years ago the possibilities of combination were not so great as now, and the economist could more

[1] "Logical Method," p. 42.

safely leave it out of account; but Adam Smith noticed the tendency even at that time: " People of the same trade hardly ever meet together, even for merriment and diversion, but the conversation ends in a conspiracy against the public." [1] Mill, too, recognized the imperfect action of competition, and devoted a chapter [2] to an exposition of these imperfections; at the same time warning the reader that "these observations [about the occasional absence of competition] must be received as a general correction to be applied whenever relevant, whether expressly mentioned or not, to the conclusions contained in the subsequent portions of this treatise." [3] One of the most notable advances of economic science in recent years—Cairnes's doctrine of non-competing groups—starts from the recognition of certain limitations on the

[1] Quoted by H. D. Lloyd, in *North American Review*, vol. cxxxviii., p. 565. Whoever would learn the extent to which combination has already taken place in our leading pursuits should turn to this article of Mr. Lloyd's on the " Lords of Industry."
[2] " Principles of Political Economy," Book II., chap. iv.
[3] " Principles," etc. (Laughlin's edition), p. 177.

action of competition. Not to multiply examples unduly, suffice it to say that English economics, in theory and in practice alike, is opposed to any thing like an exclusive dependence upon competition.

Another criticism persistently urged by Historical writers against English economics relates to the attitude of the English school toward the doctrine of *laissez-faire*. This doctrine, it is argued, has been proved an unsafe principle for the guidance of the statesman, has not been consistently carried out even in England, and is clearly impotent in the presence of the labor question, railroad supervision, and other modern problems. Now, all this may be or may not be true; without presuming to pass judgment upon that, and without attempting any defence of the doctrine of non-interference, we would simply direct attention here to the fact that criticisms of this sort aimed at the English school are plainly beside the point—supposing the point to be the one usual in such cases, that is, the condemnation of English economics as a science of the laws of wealth. Economics, purely as such, has nothing to do with theories about governmental functions ; and English economists, as such, are not bulwarked in favor of *laissez-faire* or any other " handy rule of practice."[1] It is conceivable, of course,—even reasonable to suppose,—that an economist will be led, by the teachings of his science, to have a definite opinion about the advisability of governmental interference. Adam Smith, for example, viewing the commercial legislation of the eighteenth century in the light afforded by the laws of political economy, made a sweeping attack upon the prevailing theories, and gave the doctrine of individual sufficiency a fundamental place in his system of applied economics. But the industrial world has changed vastly since 1776, and in a way that affects the consideration of this question. While Adam Smith was laying

[1] This is the phrase by which Cairnes describes the doctrine of *laissez-faire* (" Essays, Theoretical and Applied," p. 244). In the same way Professor F. W. Taussig calls the doctrine a "rough rule of thumb" (" Science Economic Discussion," p. 35).

the deep and broad foundation upon which the economic structure has risen to its present imposing dimensions, Arkwright and Hargreaves were making possible the textile industries of to-day. During the same year James Watt was beginning to realize the marvellous possibilities of his discovery; and the sale of the first steam-engine synchronizes with the publication of the "Wealth of Nations." About the same time, too, experiments were going on at Coalbrookdale and at other mining centres in England, that were to pave the way for the modern iron industry. In short, the industrial world, as it exists to-day, with all its dangerous possibilities, was just shaping itself, when economics sprung forth, Athena-like, in the "Wealth of Nations." Under the changed conditions of the modern world, perhaps the doctrine of the economic passivity of the state may be pushed too far. The factory system, carrying with it a minute division of labor unfavorable to intellectual vigor or to mental development, has succeeded the cottage industries of a century ago;

gigantic, spongily absorbent transportation companies, in vital connection with the industrial life of the community, have no prototype in the economic world of one hundred years ago; sin-breeding and health-sapping coagulations of humanity, constantly menacing the political welfare of our cities, have taken the place of the idyllic group formed by the weaver and his children about the household loom; a well-equipped and highly-organized army of laborers, exalted with conquest and more aggressive daily, has succeeded the servile workman, a legal industrial slave, cringing before his overseer.

Plainly enough, there are more things now than in 1776 that cannot safely be left to private initiative: and the recognition of this fact is quite consistent with the endorsement of Adam Smith's political economy. We shall have to recur to this matter shortly in connection with another aspect of the Historical school of economists: the thing to be noted here is that the doctrine of *laissez-faire* forms no essential part of the English economics, and that, accordingly, criticisms deriving their force from the identification of the English school with one or another view as to governmental interference are valueless as criticisms, because aside from the purpose in hand.

The foregoing are, perhaps, the leading objections raised by the new school against the old economics. But some Historical writers seem to think that no good thing can come out of English economics; and we have, accordingly, in addition to these fundamental strictures, a choice assortment of minor criticisms so varied and comprehensive in character that their validity would imply the complete obliteration of the old political economy. Moreover, not content with crying down what has been done, Historical writers denounce the old school for what has not been done; and it is a question with some critics whether these sins of omission do not overtop in iniquity even the positive transgressions of the older economics.[1] But time would

[1] Cliffe Leslie, for example, calls the English school to ac-

Economical Science. 73

fail the writer, as patience would fail the reader, if the attempt should be made to portray in full this negative side of the new economics. Without delaying longer, therefore, on this attitude of the Historical school, let us turn to the positive side of that school,—let us consider the new principles and the new conceptions that are to take the place of the older doctrines.

count for having " neglected the important department of the consumption of wealth " (" Essays in Political and Moral Philosophy," p. 155); though one is at a loss to understand what the English school could put into that department beyond an historical account of the course that consumption usually takes in growing communities. It is a great pity, by the way, that Mr. Leslie did not supply some of the many deficiencies that he found in the current doctrines. If he had replaced a small part of what he attempted to tear down, the economic edifice would now be a marvel of architectural elegance. A writer in the *Atlantic Monthly* (Sept., 1882) laments Mr. Leslie's " captious and quibbling " criticisms, and, evidently believing in the theory that temper is a mere matter of digestion, ascribes Mr. Leslie's conduct to ill-health.

VI.

THE POSITIVE SIDE OF THE NEW SCHOOL.

The chief characteristic of the new school is indicated by one of its names, and consists in the great prominence given to historical investigation. The fact that "a people is not merely the mass of individuals now living" is deemed by Roscher a point of pivotal importance in economics; and Hildebrand lays equal stress on the circumstance that "man, as a member of society, is a child of civilization and a product of history": while both Roscher and Hildebrand, as well as Historical economists in general, infer from these facts that the study and comparison of history, especially economic history, should be the chief business of economists.

Some one has said that history, so far as it is a mere chronicle of events, is no more a science than a city directory: and

Economical Science. 75

we have already noticed[1] the utter inadequacy of one "historical method" in economics; that, namely, which is adopted by Schmoller, and which resolves itself into a mere recording of economic events and accumulation of statistical knowledge. Such work is, of course, a part—and a very essential part—of any scientific method of studying the phenomena of wealth; but it is difficult to see that such work is anything more than a part of a method. To study economics with sole reliance upon this means would be like studying astronomy by simply recording celestial phenomena without attempting to interpret them by the aid of the laws of gravitation and of motion.

Dismissing, then, this "historical method"—the more readily because it is repudiated by the majority of the new school—we come to the less extreme method, which, admitting the necessity of a philosophic analysis of the motives and a systematic formulation of the principles that underlie the economic world, deems mere

[1] *Ante*, pp. 53, 54.

historical research insufficient, and supplements this by deductive reasoning. Wagner, perhaps, represents as well as any one this more rational conception of an historical method in economics; and this is the way that he describes the proper relation between induction and deduction in economic inquiry: "Induction must always be brought to aid in making more accurate the approximate conclusions which have been reached by deduction, and which, as a rule, can be reached by deduction alone. . . . These, then, are the two methods: on the one hand, deduction from psychological motives,—first and foremost, deduction from the motive of individual advantage, then from the other motives; on the other hand, induction from history, from statistics, and from the less exact and less certain, yet indispensable, process of common observation and experience." [1]

Professor Cairnes himself could hardly have made, in the same compass, a more

[1] Translated in the *Quarterly Journal of Economics*, No. 1, p. 124.

accurate statement of the English method than that just quoted from Wagner; and whether or not the average economist of the new school would accept Wagner's method in its entirety, we must contend that the difference between the old and the new school, as regards the importance of historical investigation, is a difference of degree only. The old economics, to be sure, shrinks from certain excesses of the new method in the use of history. English economists, for example, have little sympathy with the idea that they should go on for several years to come, piling up historic material, before attempting to give this material scientific form. So, too, the old school cannot quite agree with Roscher that "all the peoples from whom we can learn any thing must be studied and compared from the economic point of view, especially the ancient peoples, whose development lies before us in its totality." Say conjectured that if Carthage, with its highly developed commerce, had gained the upper hand in the struggle with Rome, economics might have received from the ancient world the same impetus that other branches of knowledge owe to the Renaissance. As it is, however, antiquity has contributed little or nothing to economics; and the utterly unlike conditions of the ancient and the modern economic world make one question the wisdom of Roscher's view.[1]

From these and a few other extravagances of the Historical method, English economists hold themselves aloof. Nevertheless, the English method presupposes the constant use of history, and might indeed, without any straining of language, be called "historical." When the English economist has drawn certain conclusions from his time-tested premises, he proceeds to complete his work by confronting these conclusions with the actual course of affairs as shown by historic investigation: and it is only after such conclusions have been thus confirmed or cor-

[1] In an excellent article on the history of economic thought Dr. Edwin R. A. Seligman shows that economics among the ancients was impossible, because "the whole environment was of a nature to preclude speculation of this kind." See "'Science Economic Discussion," pp. 4–7.

rected—possibly confuted—that the English method has been fully carried out.

In the case of many practical problems in economics, where the lack of trustworthy data throws doubt upon the deductive conclusions, this historical part of the process is by far the more important; and the English economists have shown their appreciation of this fact by the way in which they have taken such problems in hand. Adam Smith is praised on all sides for his efficient use of history in clinching deductive arguments, and Cliffe Leslie goes so far as to claim the Glasgow professor as an Historical economist. Malthus arrived at his famous doctrine by speculative reasoning; but he felt it necessary to ransack the earth for historic illustrations and confirmations of his theory. English economics attacks the land-holding problem first by the way of deduction; but Mill and Fawcett and other English economists were content with nothing less than an exhaustive study of the French and Belgian peasantry. *A priori* economics easily infers, from a premise supplied by the history of labor-saving machinery, that the condition of the laborer has been much improved in the last half century; but a Giffen and an Edward Atkinson were needed to complete the demonstration. English political economy, as might be expected from the character of its logical method, abounds in just such examples of combined historic and speculative treatment of economic questions.

As regards, then, the solution of particular problems in economics, there is no doubt as to the usefulness of an historical method—that is, a method in which historical investigation shall play an important part. Yet even here it is only a part of the process that history furnishes; and we must still resort to those fundamental premises of the science that are applicable to a vast range of problems, and that guide our steps throughout the domain of the economic world. As for these fundamental premises, the more important of them may be framed without the aid of history; and the others depend upon historical research only as most economic conclusions depend upon such research—that is, in the way of confirmation and possible correction.

Professor Richmond M. Smith, however, contends that the historical method is capable by itself of formulating general principles to which particular problems may be referred. From the history of the double standard, for example, Historical economists derive a general principle commonly known as Gresham's law. But the English economists reach the same principle by a simple mental process; though they welcome such work as Professor Laughlin's study of bimetallism as a striking and necessary confirmation of their deductive conclusions. Another example that Professor Smith gives to illustrate the way in which history furnishes economics with general principles must be regarded as somewhat unfortunate : " From the prosperity of England [we reason] to the theory of free-trade." [1]

[1] "Science Economic Discussion," p. 113. To what, then, do they reason from the prosperity of this country or from the pre-eminence of England fifty years ago? The fallacy of "*post hoc ergo propter hoc*" is nowhere better illustrated

Even if we admit that historical investigation, when carried far enough and inter-

than in this matter of protection and free trade. In former times protectionists pointed to the example of England in the same conclusively exultant manner with which free-traders to-day accompany the same act. An extreme example of this style of argument is afforded by those who ascribe the backward condition of Turkey to the commercial policy adopted by that country—an exhibition of "sweet reasonableness" that is, to say the least of it, sufficiently smile-stirring. Hardly less absurd, however, are some interpretations of history to which the tortuous course of our own tariff legislation has given rise. The commercial depression of the years 1837–41 is perfectly explained in Carey's mind by the "compromise tariff" act of 1833, although the operation of this act did not bring about any considerable reduction in the tariff charges until the elements of prosperity in the business world were at hand. Carey had a most curious incapacity for impartial reasoning, and the history that he read was highly colored by his pre-conceived opinions. We need not wonder, then, at his interpretation of these years; the remarkable thing is that he should have been followed in this regard by later writers—by Stebbins and Thompson and Bolles. On the other hand, free-traders, it must be said, have shown as little reason in ascribing to the tariff act of 1846 the general prosperity of this country in the following years.

All attempts of this sort to connect general business conditions with a particular tariff policy must be made with the greatest care. Of course, the commercial policy adopted by a great nation cannot fail to have important consequences in the industrial history of that nation: but scores of other things have as much and more importance: and to ascribe the general resultant effect to a single one of the contributing causes is to violate the commonest rules of logic.

Economical Science. 83

preted with the utmost caution, may lead to generalizations of sufficient importance to constitute subordinate premises available for economic reasoning, the fact will remain that the chief resource of the economist lies in the recognition of those ever-relevant principles that so largely concern the production and the distribution of wealth : and these classical "mental principles and physical conditions" are, as we have said, beyond the reach of the purely historical method.

How essential these premises are in economic reasoning may be seen from the practice of the "inductive" economists themselves : for, however much Historical writers have derided " *a priori* reasoning," and have deprecated the use of " premature assumptions," the same writers have constantly used this identical reasoning, and have not scrupled to avail themselves, wherever possible, of these same assumptions with a serene disregard of their immaturity. Indeed, the latest statement of the new methods distinctly appropriates this feature of the old economics : " There is absolutely nothing in the new method," says[1] Richmond M. Smith, "to prevent our accepting and using any facts of the human mind or of nature which will aid us in determining how men act in economic affairs": and, to be sure, there is nothing to prevent this—except the use of the word "new."

We found just now Adam Smith, Malthus, Mill, and the English economists generally making a constant use of history; and the writers of the Historical school have sometimes[2] used the examples thus afforded to prove the excellence of the *new* method. No one can deny that this is one way of looking at the question; but most people would conclude, rather, that the new method, so far as its historical aspect is concerned, is not new at all—unless increased emphasis be deemed a sufficient title to novelty. Whether or not this accentuation of the importance of

[1] "Science Economic Discussion," p. 113.
[2] Cf. Cliffe Leslie in numerous instances, Stanley Jevons's speech at the Smith centenary dinner, and Professor Smith's article, "Methods of Investigation," etc., in the brochure so often referred to here, "Science Economic Discussion."

historical research in economics was called for by the practice of the English economists is a question that need not detain us here. It may well be that this note of warning was needed to mortify the taste of the average economist for abstract speculation; and, so far as this is so, the new movement must be credited with good work. The fact remains, however, that we have here not a radical departure from old methods, but only a criticism— a notable and necessary criticism, if you will—of existing methods; there is no sufficient basis here for a new school.

In some other respects, however, the divergence between the old and the new view of economic methods and aims is more marked; and we have a case in point in that article of the new faith which insists upon the perfect mutuality of the social sciences, and which, accordingly, merges political economy in the larger science of sociology. Here again the two schools go hand in hand for a part of the way; and we shall do well to note the exact point at which they part company.

That the general science of sociology is made up of several closely interrelated parts, of which economics is one, has never been disputed by the English economists. On the contrary, the latter have emphasized this interdependence of the social sciences, and have always maintained that the application of economic truths presupposes the proper correlation of those truths with the teachings of jurisprudence and politics and ethics. What English economists venture to deny is, that certain elements in this aggregate social condition—the elements with which economics has to do—are not best considered by themselves apart from the other forms of social speculation. So vast is the field of general sociology, so varied are the interests appurtenant to different parts of that field, so diverse are the aspects under which the same facts of society must be viewed in different lines of social study—political, ethical, jural, economic,—so contradistinct, in fine, are the various branches of social inquiry, that the English economists count it a distinct gain to isolate as completely as possible the class of phenomena with which they are concerned, and view the introduction of extra-economic considerations as a gratuitous complication of their problems.

Not so, however, the latter-day economists. So far as sociology is concerned, they do not hesitate to "drive the sciences abreast," nor do they despair of "reducing all knowledge into harmony." English economists, as we have seen, admit—or, rather, maintain—that the social sciences are tightly dovetailed together, and that, accordingly, the correct interpretation of economic truths implies a certain correlation with associated facts. But Historical economists go a step beyond this and declare that the connection between economics and the related sciences is simply umbilical. Each branch of social science, they say, is grafted into the general sociological trunk beyond the possibility of severance; and, more especially, the facts of wealth—the various phenomena connoted in the word economic—are so inseparably intertwined around moral and juristic facts, and economic laws are so rigidly conditioned by the other laws of man's social nature, that the discovery of sound principles is impossible with any method not based on this organic nature of the economic life.

Stated in these general terms this argument is not without a certain degree of plausibility; and those who favor this view are careful not to forfeit their vantage-ground by descending into particulars. Current explanations in economics, it is said, are weakened by the narrowness of the pedestal on which they rest; and true explanations are possible only when the premises are co-extensive with the plane of social life; but what particular doctrine of the current economics is so enfeebled, and what new explanation illustrates the better method —this part of the demonstration is less easy to find.

The advantage in limiting the field of economics and the effectiveness of the

"Orthodox" way of attacking social problems are shown by the whole history of pure and applied economics. A simple illustration will make the method clear. It is proposed to change the working-day from ten to eight hours; the problem is to determine whether or not this change should be made. At the first blush there throng upon the mind a crowd of considerations based on different principles, of varying degrees of importance, and leading to opposite conclusions. The first thing to do, then, is to set in order this confused body of opinion, so that arguments looking in one direction may be weighed with those indicating a different conclusion; and this end is reached by resolving the problem into its various elements and treating each of these separately.

The question obviously has an economic side; and we may first inquire what political economy has to say about the matter. The workman will produce less in eight hours than in ten—probably not so much as a fifth less, but certainly somewhat less; the average share of each consumer will be smaller; the aggregate wealth of the country will increase less rapidly; and capital will grow more slowly. Economics says this, and steps aside in favor of ethics. The latter finds in the added leisure of the laborer a chance for new pleasures (some of them noxious, no doubt), for needed recreation, and for intellectual and spiritual development. So far as the moral nature is concerned, the proposed change will, on the whole, make life better worth living for a large part of the community. After contributing so much to the solution of the problem the ethical philosopher gives way to the political philosopher or the statesman. The latter uses the data furnished by his predecessors, weighs the comparative advantages in the two results—the accumulation of wealth on the one hand, and the growth of the civic virtues on the other— and makes a decision accordingly.

Where is the error in this process, and where is the danger in separating thus the various parts of the problem? Is it not true that the laborer will produce less in eight hours than in ten ; and why not, then, single out this fact, and be sure of so much, at least, in the general maze presented by every social question ? Is it not equally clear that the ethical side of the case favors the proposed change ; and should we not, then, take this fact by itself, and to that extent simplify the issue? We may certainly plead the analogy of the physical sciences in defence of this view ; for the whole history of physics shows that progress has been made only by narrowing, in just this way, the field of investigation. Admitting that the example of the physical sciences is against them, Historical economists contend that the greater complexity of the social sciences differentiates the case. But how can this be so, in view of the fact that, even in the case of the physical sciences, the great reason for specialization is the confusion that would otherwise ensue ? If the social sciences are more complex, there would seem to be all the more reason for splitting up resultant phenomena into their various elements, so that the effect of each force may be more accurately measured.

"You have founded an entire science of political economy," says Ruskin[1] to the English economists, "on what you have stated to be the constant instinct of man—the desire to defraud his neighbor": and Henry C. Carey, long before the Historical school was thought of, charged economics with "having made for itself a being which it denominated man, from whose composition it excluded all those parts of man that are common to him and the angels, retaining carefully all those common to him and the beasts of the forest."[2] These passages strike a responsive chord in the teachings of the new economics; for Historical economists agree with Sissy-Jupe in "Hard Times" that the first principle of

[1] Whoever has read the economic works of the great art-critic will agree with Bagehot that Ruskin had "a mind of contrary flexure, whose particular bent it is to contradict what others around them say." Even in this pun-discrediting age we may pardon a witty reviewer of Ruskin, who declared that, in view of the Latin proverb, "Unto This Last" would more properly have been called "*Beyond His Last.*"

[2] "Social Science" (McKean edition), p. 103.

political economy is the golden rule. That the ethical element should not predominate in economics is an idea at which their moral sense revolts ; and Emerson seems to them to have said something, when he declared that the "best political economy is the care and culture of men."

From the fervent language of some critics one would infer that the attitude of the English school toward ethics implied a certain presumption of moral iniquity on the part of those who take the "Orthodox" view : but I suppose we need not linger over this phase of the question. As we have seen elsewhere, English economists do not think of applying economic truths without first taking into account the moral aspects of the case ; and where the two considerations clash, English economists never dream of making the moral element subservient to the economic. The sooner a boy begins to work, the more he will produce, and the greater will be the wealth of the country ; so that compulsory education for the young could hardly exist, if pure economics were allowed to settle the question. In a multitude of cases like this economic considerations have to give way to the higher issues involved.

Thus, the English school does not overlook ethical considerations, but only keeps them in reserve, until they can be introduced without danger of vitiating the results of purely economic reasoning. This proposed " reunion of ethics with political economy " is really only another aspect of that side of the Historical school that we have just considered : and the same considerations that gave us pause before attempting to treat in the lump a heterogeneous mass of social questions pluck us by the sleeve when we try to combine moral and economic interests within the limits of a single line of study. The two kinds of investigation are incompatible—from the nature of the case they cannot be combined. The various things concerned in the production and the distribution of wealth must be classified in one way for the purposes of economic investigation, in quite a different way for the purposes of ethical study. The famous divine, whose heaven-inspired words transport a multitude of hearers every week, receives a salary determined by the same principle that regulates the pay of the prize-fighter. In this respect, then, economics must place these persons in the same category: and any method that changes this arrangement will, so far forth, result in error. The footpad who robs a man of money, and devotes the sum thus obtained to reproductive employment, "saves," just as much as the poor seamstress who, at the expense of health and comfort, garners up the same amount from her pitiful stipend: that is, the word "saves" in economics has no moral connotation. English economists are held up to ridicule, because in their eyes "a pot of beer and a picture— a book of religion and a pack of cards— are equally objects of regard": but why not, if the last phrase means only, "are equally objects of value"? For certain purposes,—*e. g.*, for the purposes of the economist in search of the law underlying the value of commodities—these various objects are "equally worthy of regard";

and any method of investigation that proceeds on a different principle will only make poor ethics out of good economics. That a pot of beer and a pack of cards have value, is a fact: and to disregard facts or to do any thing other than accept and act upon them, is not the part of true science. To be sure, it is not always easy to do this: according to Professor Simon Newcomb, "one of the most difficult pieces of mental discipline is that of learning to look upon facts simply as facts"[1]; but every scientist—above all, every social scientist—must acquire this discipline, and must use facts as he finds them, whether or not such as he would like them to be.

We have already found the new economists disclaiming belief in *laissez-faire* and criticising the English school for a supposed devotion to that doctrine; and we come now to a positive principle of the new school that is correlative to this negative feature—that idea of the economic function of the state that we embody in

[1] "Science Economic Discussion," p. 62.

the phrase, "paternal government." We need not consider at length this aspect of the new economics ; for the application of economic truths is a matter quite distinct from the question of scientific method, and can hardly be made the basis of opposing schools of political economy. Just as the maxim of *laissez-faire* forms no part of pure economics, but is, as Professor Cairnes says, a "mere handy rule of practice, totally destitute of all scientific authority"[1]; so the opposite doctrine, with which the new economists identify themselves, is really no part of economic science, and would more properly characterize a school of politicians than a school of economists. Whether or not Historical economists are wise in calling for increased governmental interference is an interesting and fruitful inquiry ; but the scope of this essay forbids any extended discussion of the subject.

[1] "Essays," etc., p. 244. In view of the danger that often lurks in short quotations, I may add that Professor Cairnes is by no means to be regarded as an advocate of state-control. He repudiates the scientific authority of *laissez-faire ;* but he insists upon the great practical value of the doctrine as a guide for the statesman.

Dr. Seligman reminds [1] us that the "practical conclusions [of economics] must not be dissociated from the shifting necessities of the age"; and probably not many people would deny that the "necessities of the age," as regards state intervention, have shifted in the course of the present century. How far this change will justify us in going is, however, a matter more open to doubt. Unquestionably, the spirit of the times would carry us a long way in the direction of governmental tutelage. This tendency is world-wide; but the course of history in our own country has aggravated the tendency here in a peculiar way. The exigencies of the civil war led Congress to assume greater and greater authority; and the drift of affairs during the period of reconstruction was in the same direction. Already we have reached the point at which the State takes upon itself the enforcement of sanitary regulations, a limited restraint of corporations, and a certain oversight of production and transportation. Even as I write, the law-

" [1] Science Economic Discussion," p. 22.

Economical Science.

makers of Massachusetts are considering a measure by which the State is to arbitrate between the clashing interests of employer and employee; and Congress is on the point of passing a bill that will give to the national government a more effective control of commerce.

There is, of course, nothing very portentous in all this; but the elements of danger are present none the less. Some one has said that the goal toward which mankind has been struggling for the last two thousand years is that of personal freedom; and certainly one of the purposes running through the ages has been this development of individual liberty. Yet the doctrine of state-control is directly opposed to individuality, and tends to repress spontaneity of character. μηδὲν ἄγαν —" do nothing too much "—was a favorite maxim with the proportion-loving Greeks; and perhaps the time has already come when these words have a meaning for those who would lead us still further toward paternalism in government. At all events, thoughtful men, who are not carried away by the spirit of the age, or who, like Lowell, have become distrustful of that sign from having lived to see "several spirits of the age guiding in different directions," are beginning to sound a note of alarm. Woodrow Wilson notices the tendencies in this country favoring a centralization of governmental functions, and finds the national government concerning itself with things that "do not lie even within the enlarged sphere of the federal government, and can be embraced within its jurisdiction only by wresting the Constitution to strange and yet unimagined uses."[1] A still more authoritative warning comes from Mr. John Fiske, who sees grave danger in that phase of paternal government with which this country is threatened: "Too much centralization is our danger to-day, as the weakness of the federal tie was our danger a century ago. . . . If the day should ever arrive (which God forbid!) when the people of different parts of our country shall allow their local affairs to be administered by

---

[1] "Congressional Government," p. 54.

prefects sent from Washington, and when the self-government of the States shall have been so far lost as that of the departments of France, or even so far as that of the departments of England—on that day the progressive political career of the American people will have come to an end, and the hopes that have been built upon it for the future happiness and prosperity of mankind will have been wrecked forever." [1]

[1] *Atlantic Monthly*, vol. lix., p. 228.

VII.

THE RESULTS OF OUR STUDY.

What, then, is the outcome of our long investigation into the methods and the doctrines of the new economists? In the first place, a large part of the new political economy, we have seen, is made up of mere criticism—and criticism, too, for the most part, not of English economics, but of certain extravagant and wholly unwarranted misconceptions of the English economics. Then, as for the constructive side of the new school, we have found that in essential features this aspect of the school is not new; and so far as, in a few details, the school is new,—so far as it attempts impossible things, or mixes matters best considered apart, or espouses political movements of doubtful expediency,—so far it would better have remained old. The conclusion of the whole matter seems to be that the new school really has no reason for existence.

It is by their works, after all, that we must know economists; and the foregoing conclusion is not weakened, when we subject the new school to the test of actual results. As for the services of the English economists, it would hardly be too much to say that the whole science of political economy, as it is to-day, is the work of their hands. M. Comte, indeed, declares that the results of political economy are "radically sterile"; and so they are, perhaps, as compared with the possible results. Granting, however, that we do not know much as yet about the laws of wealth; still, the little that we do know must be credited to the English economists. Nor can we deem even this little of slight importance, if we remember what economic legislation was a century ago. The Swedish statesman, Oxenstiern, sending his son to foreign courts, bade him observe with how little wisdom the world was governed; and this observation was easily made before the rise of English economics. Cairnes calls [1] London "a mighty monument of economic achievement"; and Bagehot declares [2] that the teachings of political economy have settled down into the common-sense of the English people, ideas that are paradoxes everywhere else having become axioms in England. The marvellous progress of Great Britain since 1776 shows at every step the influence of the "Wealth of Nations" [3]; and each advance in economic knowledge since Smith's time has been

[1] "Essays," etc., p. 232.
[2] "Economic Studies," p. 1.
[3] Few social reformers have so quickly secured recognition as Adam Smith. Already well known from his earlier writings, Smith found an eager public awaiting the publication of his long-maturing views; and the "Wealth of Nations" began almost immediately to affect public opinion, and especially the more authoritative part of public opinion. Buckle estimates Smith's influence by the number of times that the "Wealth of Nations" was cited in Parliament. According to tradition, Adam Smith declared that Pitt knew the "Wealth of Nations" better than the author himself knew the book, and it is certain that the great statesman owed many of his economic convictions to the Glasgow professor. The commercial treaty between France and England in 1786 was based on ideas far in advance of those commonly held at that time; and the fact that leading legislators in both countries were willing to breast a strong current of opposition for the sake of carrying through this treaty shows how far Smith's

quickly turned to account in promoting England's commercial greatness. The balance of trade theory, the navigation laws, and the colonial policy[1] were among the first things to feel the effect of the more liberal ideas of commerce ; and free trade, the poor-law system, and a multitude of fiscal reforms are later achievements of the English economics.

What have the new economists done to compare with all this ? What people have they indoctrinated with new ideas ?

views had been taken up by influential men. In our own country Hamilton's remarkable economic writings plainly show an acquaintance with the " Wealth of Nations " ; and many members of the Convention of 1787 were familiar with the book.

[1] Besides Adam Smith, Lord Sheffield, Sinclair, Arthur Young, and others combated the English colonial policy, advising a general emancipation of colonies. But the speculations of these "closeted theorists" would probably have availed little with the " practical " statesmen of England, had it not been for the example afforded by the American colonies. Seeing from her experience with this country that colonies should be managed with a view to their best interests, England completely altered her system, making her colonies virtually independent. This change has been of the first importance to England. It is difficult to see how Canada and Australia, which hold so important a place in England's commercial relations, could have secured, under the old system, their present development.

What economic reform have they effected? What important principle underlying the phenomena of wealth have they discovered? Indirectly, indeed, their work has not been in vain. They have emphasized the importance of historical research in economic method; and even well-known truths will bear repetition. They have subjected fundamental principles to searching criticism; and this is always a real service. Moreover, as regards direct assistance, they have given us great volumes of statistics of more or less value; and individual economists have thrown light upon particular problems. These things, if we mistake not, constitute the sum of the benefits conferred by the new school upon political economy.

It is not difficult to forecast the issue of this contest between the schools. Already the two sides are weary of the struggle, and are casting about for some means of reconciliation. Every one recognizes the discredit that attaches to the science from this lack of harmony among economists. One observer is filled with pity to see men thus wasting their energy in arguing, as the Greeks would have said, about the shadow of an ass. Treitschke calls the quarrel a wind-mill fight. Sensible men long ago dropped the controversy, and went about their business, careless as to whether their methods were called "Historical" or "Orthodox." The later and more approved statements of the new method discover no essential differences from the old.[1] The English method has

[1] Francis A. Walker, after giving an abstract of Cairnes's statement of the English method, continues ("Political Economy," p. 15): "Nothing could be added to this admirable statement of Political Economy according to the so-called German school." Dr. Seligman formulates the leading principles of the new economics in this way ("Science Econ. Discussion," p. 19): "1. It discards the exclusive use of the deductive method, and intonates the necessity of historical and statistical treatment. 2. It denies the existence of immutable natural laws in economics, calling attention to the interdependence of theories and institutions, and showing that the different epochs or countries require different systems. 3. It disclaims belief in the beneficence of the absolute *laissez-faire* system; it maintains the close interrelation of law, ethics, and economics; and it refuses to acknowledge the adequacy of a scientific explanation, based on the assumption of self-interest as the sole regulator of economic action." Dr. Seligman calls these the principles of the new economics; but the old economics "discards the exclusive use of the deductive method," "denies the existence of immutable

been severely tried, and has been found able to stand the test. The new school has pointed out possible dangers in the English method, and has protested against a careless disregard of those dangers. When this point shall have been sufficiently emphasized, there will be nothing to prevent the new economists from leaguing themselves with the English school in firm alliance against the ever-growing host of economic problems.

How numerous and how grave these problems are need not be told here: for they crowd upon us at every step, and their danger is apparent at a single glance. They stand out in bold relief from the columns of every newspaper; they confront us daily in the world of business; they lie in wait behind the political movements of the time. So far from having done its work, economics, we should say, rather, is just beginning its mission. What a for-

natural laws in economics "—in fact, does every one of the things enumerated above. One cannot help thinking that the new economists resemble the French people, who, according to a nice observer, do not know what they want, and are never satisfied until they get it.

midable array of problems stare our statesmen in the face! Industrial and political "deals" and "bosses" are a constant menace to law and order; inflation schemes and a false silver dollar hang over our monetary legislation like a Damoclesian sword; unscrupulous "rings" and corrupt municipal governments threaten the stability of republican institutions; uniting workmen and consolidating capitalists keep the industrial world in continual ferment; paper-money and the banking questions, Chinese labor and general immigration, railroad control and postal telegraph, merchant shipping, giant monopolies, socialism, tariff reform—where will the list end? —all press forward for immediate attention.

Some of these are old questions, which, as James Russell Lowell says, the "sphinx of political and social economy who sits by the roadside has been proposing to mankind from the beginning, and which mankind have shown such a singular talent for answering wrongly": but many of them are new and untried problems, that follow in the train of steam and electricity and congested populations. Whether new or old, these questions in many cases present difficulties well-nigh insuperable; and in every case call for the exercise of the highest faculties of man. Well might Themistocles boast that, though he could not play on any stringed instrument, he could make, out of a little village, a great and glorious city; in some respects it seems harder now than ever to make a city that shall be glorious as well as great.

Bad as the case appears from a hasty glance, closer inspection makes the outlook hardly less portentous. The condition of the best solution of these and other problems is the diffusion of sound economic ideas among the people. What with newspapers, primers, hand-books, and pamphlets much has been done in recent years to popularize political economy; but vastly more remains to be done. "Delusions, especially economical delusions," says Lowell, "seem the only things that have any chance of an earthly immortality": and many a venerable fallacy, that was bowed down with age in the days of Adam Smith, shows its hoary front to-day in numerous articles of popular faith. Nor is it the people only that show the lack of economic training. Simon Newcomb's experience of thirty years makes him conclude that "no really wise economic legislation by Congress is attainable"[1]; and whoever has waded through the fallacy-reeking pages of the *Congressional Record* can understand this opinion.

Our indifference in the past to economic science is the more surprising from the exceptional character of our national history; for the development of this country in the last one hundred years has offered very unusual advantages for the study of economics. Commanding the markets of the world in four great staple commodities —cotton, tobacco, petroleum, the cereals, —and possessed of unrivalled facilities for the production of other leading articles of consumption, the United States has risen rapidly to a position almost first among commercial nations. Inexhaustible min-

[1] "Science Econ. Discussion," p. 65.

eral deposits, cheap food, abundant capital, skilful and energetic labor, marvellous organizing and executive ability—all are here; so that whether or not we adopt the system that will most quickly develop these resources, the time must soon come when this country will lead the world in commercial standing. Moreover, the nature of our political institutions, as well as our material progress, has made this country a promising field for economic study: for the unfettered condition of industrial elements here brings out more clearly than elsewhere the normal operation of economic forces.

Under these conditions one might have supposed that economic science would be cultivated here as nowhere else. Such, however, has not been the case. We have been so busy in producing and distributing wealth that we have found no time to consider the laws underlying these operations. Just now, indeed, we seem to be on the verge of a veritable renaissance of economic learning; but the movement is of recent origin. Cliffe Leslie a few years ago noticed[1] the slight progress of economics here; and Professor C. F. Dunbar found that, up to 1876, at least, the United States had "done nothing toward developing the theory of political economy, notwithstanding their vast and immediate interests in its practical applications."[2]

Thus we see that, here in America, at any rate, economists can ill afford to waste their energies in discussing theoretical refinements of method. They should rather husband all their resources for the purpose of grappling more successfully with questions that are at once pressing and outstandingly difficult. Happily, the few younger economists here who are pleased to call themselves Historical writers, are not prevented thereby from using the English method, as though they were to the manner born: and "Orthodox" results by any other name are just as good.

Nor is it in America only that economists would do well to turn from questions of method to the many practical problems

---

[1] *Fortnightly Review*, vol. xxxiv., p. 488.
[2] *North American Review*, January, 1876.

that cry out for attention. As for scientific method in economics, the time seems now to have arrived when discussion is uncalled for, and when the question may safely be left to settle itself. Of course I understand with what peculiar grace this statement comes at the end of 114 pages of such discussion. But then the very object of these pages was to demonstrate the soundness of this view of the case: and if that object has been in any degree attained, or if further discussion is any more unwarranted—even ever so little more—than it was before, perhaps these pages might have served a less useful purpose.

THE END.

QUESTIONS OF THE DAY.

1—**The Independent Movement in New York,** as an Element in the next Elections and a Problem in Party Government. By JUNIUS. Octavo, paper 75
2—**Free Land and Free Trade.** The Lessons of the English Corn-Laws Applied to the United States. By SAMUEL S. COX. Octavo, cloth 75
3—**Our Merchant Marine.** How it rose, increased, became great, declined, and decayed; with an inquiry into the conditions essential to its resuscitation and prosperity. By DAVID A. WELLS. Octavo, cloth 1 00
4—**The Elective Franchise in the United States.** By D. C. MCMILLAN. Octavo, cloth 1 00
5—**The American Citizen's Manual.** Edited by WORTHINGTON C. FORD. *Part I.*—Governments (National, State, and Local), the Electorate, and the Civil Service. Octavo, cloth . . 75
6—**The American Citizen's Manual.** *Part II.*—The Functions of Government, considered with special reference to taxation and expenditure, the regulation of commerce and industry, provision for the poor and insane, the management of the public lands, etc. Octavo, cloth 75
The above two volumes are also issued bound in one. Cloth . 1 25
7—**Spoiling the Egyptians.** A Tale of Shame. Told from the British Blue-Books. By J. SEYMOUR KEAY. Octavo, cloth, 75
8—**The Taxation of the Elevated Railroads in the City of New York.** By ROGER FOSTER. Octavo, paper . . . 25
9—**The Destructive Influence of the Tariff upon Manufacture and Commerce, and the Figures and Facts Relating Thereto.** By J. SCHOENHOF. Octavo, cloth, 75 cents; paper, . . 40
10—**Of Work and Wealth.** A Summary of Economics. By R. R. BOWKER. Octavo, cloth 75
11—**Protection to Young Industries as Applied in the United States.** A Study in Economic History. By F. W. TAUSSIG. Octavo, cloth 75
12—**Storage and Transportation in the Port of New York.** By W. N. BLACK. Octavo, paper 25
13—**Public Relief and Private Charity.** By JOSEPHINE SHAW LOWELL. Octavo, cloth, 75 cents; paper 40
14—**"The Jukes."** A Study in Crime, Pauperism, Disease, and Heredity. By R. L. DUGDALE. Octavo, cloth 1 00
15—**Protection and Communism.** By WM. RATHBONE. Octavo, paper 25
16—**The True Issue.** By E. J. DONNELL. Octavo, paper . . 25
17—**Heavy Ordnance for National Defence.** By WM. H. JAQUES, Lieut. U. S. Navy. Octavo, paper 25
18—**The Spanish Treaty Opposed to Tariff Reform.** By D. H. CHAMBERLAIN, JNO. DEWITT WARNER, GRAHAM MCADAM, and J. SCHOENHOF. Octavo, paper 25
19—**The History of the Present Tariff.** By F. W. TAUSSIG. Octavo, cloth 75
20—**The Progress of the Working Classes in the Last Half Century.** By ROBT. GIFFEN. Octavo, paper . . . 25

G. P. PUTNAM'S SONS, Publishers, New York and London.

QUESTIONS OF THE DAY.

21—**The Solution of the Mormon Problem.** By Capt. JOHN CODMAN. Octavo, paper 25
22—**Defective and Corrupt Legislation; the Cause and the Remedy.** By SIMON STERNE. Octavo, paper . . . 25
23—**Social Economy.** By J. E. THOROLD ROGERS. Octavo, cloth, 75
24—**The History of the Surplus Revenue of 1837.** By EDWARD G. BOURNE. Octavo, cloth 1 25
25—**The American Caucus System.** By GEORGE W. LAWTON. Octavo, cloth, $1.00 ; paper 50
26—**The Science of Business.** By RODERICK H. SMITH. 8vo, cloth, 1 25
27—**The Evolution of Revelation.** By JAMES MORRIS WHITON, PH.D. Octavo, paper 25
28—**The Postulates of English Political Economy.** By WALTER BAGEHOT. Octavo, cloth 1 00
29—**Lincoln and Stanton.** By Hon. W. D. KELLEY. Octavo, cloth, 50 cents ; paper 25
30—**The Industrial Situation.** By J. SCHOENHOF. Octavo, cloth, 1 00
31—**Ericsson's Destroyer.** By WM. H. JAQUES, Lieut. U. S. Navy. Octavo, paper, illustrated 50
32—**Modern Armor for National Defence.** By WM. H. JAQUES, Lieut. U. S. Navy. Octavo, paper, illustrated . . . 50
33—**The Physics and Metaphysics of Money.** By RODMOND GIBBONS. Octavo, paper 25
34—**Torpedoes for National Defence.** By WM. H. JAQUES, Lieut. U. S. Navy. Octavo, paper, illustrated . . . 50
35—**Unwise Laws.** By LEWIS H. BLAIR. Octavo, cloth, 1 00 paper 50
36—**Railway Practice.** By E. PORTER ALEXANDER. Octavo, cloth, 75
37—**American State Constitutions:** A Study of their Growth. By HENRY HITCHCOCK, LL.D. Octavo, cloth . . . 75
38—**The Inter-State Commerce Act:** An Analysis of Its Provisions. By JOHN R. DOS PASSOS. Octavo, cloth . . . 1 25
39—**Federal Taxation and State Expenses;** or, An Analysis of a County Tax-List. By W. H. JONES. Octavo, cloth . 1 00
40—**The Margin of Profits:** How Profits are now Divided ; What Part of the Present Hours of Labor can now be Spared. By EDWARD ATKINSON. Together with the Reply of E. M. CHAMBERLAIN, Representing the Labor Union, and Mr. Atkinson's Rejoinder. Cloth, 75 cents ; paper 40
41—**The Fishery Question.** A Summary of Its History and Analysis of the Issues Involved. By CHARLES ISHAM. 12mo, cloth, with Map of the Fishing Grounds. 75
42—**Bodyke:** A Chapter in the History of Irish Landlordism. By HENRY NORMAN. 8vo, cloth, illustrated . . . 75
43—**Slav or Saxon.** A Study of the Growth and Tendencies of Russian Civilization. By WM. D. FOULKE, A. M. Octavo, cloth 1 25
45—**The Old South and The New.** By HON. W. D. KELLEY. Octavo, cloth 1 25
46—**Property in Land.** An essay on the New Crusade. By HENRY WINN. Octavo, paper 40

G. P. PUTNAM'S SONS, Publishers, New York and London.

www.ingramcontent.com/pod-product-compliance
Lightning Source LLC
Chambersburg PA
CBHW020114170426
43199CB00009B/522